Stories of
God's Abundance
for a
More Joyful Life

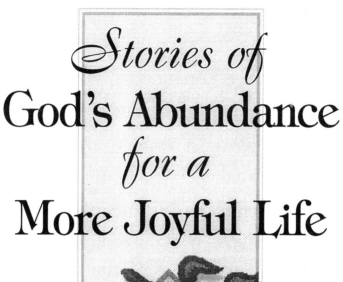

Stories of
God's Abundance
for a
More Joyful Life

COMPILED BY

Kathy Collard Miller

STARBURST PUBLISHERS®

P. O. Box 4123, Lancaster, Pennsylvania 17604

To schedule author appearances, write: Author Appearances, Starburst Promotions, P.O. Box 4123, Lancaster, Pennsylvania 17604 or call (717) 293-0939. Website: www.starburstpublishers.com.

CREDITS:
Cover design by Richmond & Williams
Text design and composition by John Reinhardt Book Design

Scripture taken from the HOLY BIBLE: NEW INTERNATIONAL VERSION®. NIV®. Copyright © 1973, 1978, 1984 by International Bible Society. Used by permission of Zondervan Publishing House. The "NIV" and "New International Version" trademarks are registered in the United States Patent and Trademark Office by International Bible Society.

To the best of its ability, Starburst Publishers® has strived to find the source of all material. If there has been an oversight, please contact us and we will make any correction deemed necessary in future printings. We also declare that to the best of our knowledge all material (quoted or not) contained herein is accurate, and we shall not be held liable for the same.

STORIES OF GOD'S ABUNDANCE

First Printing, May, 1999

ISBN: 0-892016-060
Library of Congress Catalog Number: 98-83171
Printed in the United States of America

Contents

Love

Joy

Peace

Patience

Kindness

Goodness

ℱaithfulness

Gentleness

Self-Control

Hope

Thanksgiving

Celebration

Introduction

 ometimes our spiritual eyes are just blind! God provides abundantly for our needs, gives little glimpses into His bountiful love, reveals Himself in great ways, and yet, sometimes our spiritual eyes just don't see it. In adversity, we don't see the opportunity to depend upon Him, we only view the pain. In joy, we take for granted our good fortune and fail to thank Him. In struggling relationships, we focus on changing the other person rather than being willing to change ourselves. Sometimes we just don't have the spiritual strength to see the big and little ways God is abundant in our lives.

But this book will help your eyes to see all of God's abundance. In a medley of true stories written by a variety of people, you'll be reminded that God is real, His love is abundantly unconditional, and His works surround you moment by moment. Spiritual eyes *can* be opened. Spiritual eyes *can* wear corrective glasses. Spiritual eyes *can* "get the red out!"

These touching, lovable, engaging stories of God's way in people's lives will make you more aware of how God is moving in your life. Just pick one or two each day, and your spiritual eyes will see as never before.

Love

$\mathcal{W}$e all need love and God wants us to give it away. That's why it's the most important ingredient in having an abundant life. And why God offers it so readily—because He is love in the purest form.

We love because he first loved us.

1 JOHN 4:19 (NIV)

Abundant Love
in a Little House

PATSY CLAIRMONT

*O*ur former home was a bit brief in floor space so I had to be creative to accommodate forty guests at a bridal shower for our then future daughter-in-law, Danya. I made more room by stationing my friend Carol on the porch as a greeting hostess with a water jar full of raspberry lemonade. Another friend stood at the door so that, as the guests received their drinks, she could take their gifts. The gifts were then placed on the stairwell leading up to the second floor. That gave the guests room to maneuver their way to the chairs. Our small living room was open to our tiny kitchen as was our dining room. So I put the dining room table in the office, which was off the dining room. That allowed me to set up chairs theater-style in the dining room and living room facing the kitchen. Carol and I used lace curtains to transform a kitchen stool into a princess' throne for Danya and placed it in the kitchen at a small island (draped in a crocheted tablecloth) in view of all the guests for the unwrapping of the gifts. Next to where Danya sat I floated a fragrant gardenia in an old crystal bowl with a lovely candle in a holder positioned nearby. At the close of the shower, I presented Danya's mom with the candle set to thank her for sharing her daughter (the light of her life) with our family.

The food was displayed around the perimeter of the office on antique dishes. Cut-glass cake stands presented the cheesecakes in regal style. An ultra-thin, two-foot vase featured three tall white lilies, making an elegant statement while taking up very little table space. My friend Ann loaned me charming patterned luncheon sets that the women placed in their laps as they partook of goodies.

Because we had a plan, our abbreviated space seemed more generous than it was. For that special occasion our little house handled a big memory. Yes, there's a lot to be said for small homes.

Saying "I Love You" with Burps

NORA LACIE ABELL

he telephone jangled deep into my sleepy head, pulling me toward the surface of the reality of dark, wee hours. I struggled up to my elbow, muttering calming words to my dead-to-the-world husband, and listened groggily as the answering machine picked up the call. After the familiar out-going message played, followed by the ensuing pause, a loud, prolonged burp rumbled into the receiver. I put my head back onto my familiar pillow and drifted back to sleep smiling. It was just Quentin saying "I love you."

Quentin is autistic. Small for a twelve-year old, he nevertheless carries the full weight of typically adolescent impishness, conflicting hormone-driven behavior, and a kind of silliness on those small brown shoulders. His autism isolates him in a mysterious world, little understood even by the medical community, and baffling to the rest of us. Whatever the reason behind the physiology, the strange impact on Quentin's brain is that he is pulled into a very private world, and that makes him hard to live with. He's stubborn, obsessive, contrary, and cunning. He would prefer to never talk, not look anyone in the eye, and to be allowed to have his own way, but his patient parents and sisters encourage him to communicate. And his methods are, to say the least, unique. Quentin communicates with outbursts, odd-sounding speech, and occasionally, exaggerated burping.

When we first met him, we strained to understand him. We leaned forward, thinking maybe proximity might make it easier. We gesticulated and used a semi-sign language. We asked him to repeat himself, which only made him angry. Finally, Larry just took him fishing. That's all. His midnight call to us was his way of saying he appreciated the non-judgmental love his new fishing buddy had shown him during their recent excursion. Quentin understood the encouragement and just wanted to show his gratitude. He got out of bed, found the telephone in the dark kitchen by himself, dialed our number from memory and burped out "I love you." It was up to us to understand the message.

Aren't our prayers often like that? Do we sometimes "dial up" God and basically just "burp" out a series of requests, praises, and appreciation? The most gifted Christian often feels like the autistic child: isolated, unlovable, overwhelmed by the world, unable to bond to the Creator of the universe. How could God love that?

How could He not? Suddenly, we saw ourselves as trapped as Quentin by similar constraining circumstances, limited by our senses, and desperate to communicate with our Heavenly Father. We spew our concerns. We erupt in our distresses. With His perfect wisdom, God provides an abundant interpreter for us—through His Holy Spirit! When God listens to our imperfect message in the wee hours of our prayers, He hears our love.

Theology of Basketball

STEVE FARRAR

*T*wo years ago, I was in the backyard shooting baskets with my son, Josh. Josh was five then, and hadn't really mastered the fundamentals of the game. Josh would dribble once or twice and then pick up the ball and take twenty or thirty steps before making a shot. That's okay when you're five.

A few minutes later, Rachel, who was then ten, came out and joined in. Before you knew it, my eight-year-old, John, had joined us, and we had ourselves a full-fledged game. Then my wife Mary came out and got into the action. We were all there: shooting, passing, rebounding, and traveling.

Every thirty seconds or so, Josh would get the ball, forget to dribble, and run thirty or forty yards for a touchdown. When you're five, it's hard to remember what game you're playing. We were laughing and yelling and having a great time, and then the ball bounced off of Rachel's foot and went under the deck. It took John about forty-five seconds to crawl under the deck and re-trieve the ball.

While I waited for him to get the ball, suddenly something unexpected happened. It's hard to explain, but it was as though time suddenly stood still and everything around me froze. For some reason, I saw everything before me through the lens of eter-nity. Through this lens, everything took on a different perspec-tive. I saw Josh hugging Mary's leg, I saw Rachel telling John to hurry up and get the ball, and in the quietness of my heart I paused and thought, *You know, Steve, it doesn't get any better than this.*

That evening, as I stood in the backyard and looked at my family, it hit me like a ton of bricks. This is success. *This* is happi-ness. I have been given the gift of a family and we belong to Jesus Christ. It doesn't get any better than that. And I realized it just by shooting baskets in the back yard with my family.

One day in the future, when I am seventy or seventy-five years old, I'll be sitting around the table with Mary, drinking a glass of iced tea on a beautiful spring evening, and I'll say to her, "Do you remember when we used to play basketball with the kids in the backyard? Weren't those great days?" And we'll pass the evening together, thinking of the days that we are living *now*.

The point is this: in another thirty-five years, I will be remembering the quality of our relationships. Not the things we had or didn't have, but the love and fun and tears and yelling in the back yard. That's what I'll remember.

Building Anticipation

BILL FARREL

 was having one of those days! I was working hard, and there seemed to be no break on the horizon. I knew I was going to be wrapped up with work all day, and the next two were already heavily scheduled. I love my work, but what I really wanted was to be home with Pam. I was distracted by intimate thoughts about her, and I was having a hard time concentrating on the task at hand. It occurred to me that I had to run by the house to pick up some work papers I had left on the kitchen counter, but I had only a few minutes to be home because I was up against a deadline.

I wanted Pam to know that I was distracted, but I couldn't get carried away. So I thought about what I could say to let her in on the desire of my heart as I drove toward the house. As I walked in the door to get the papers, I took time to look for her. I found her in the office, wrapped my arms around her waist, looked her confidently in the eyes, and said, "I wish I was independently wealthy and could stay home and love you all day long."

I then kissed her, picked up my papers, and headed back to work. The next couple of days were just as busy as I thought they would be. I had to leave early in the morning, and I didn't get home until I was exhausted from fourteen hours of work each day. But the third day was a different story!

I had the day off, and we had planned to get some chores done around the house. We got the kids off to school, and I started making plans to attack my chores. Pam kept following me around, acting very interested. She was saying flirty things and giggling at everything I said. She was making up reasons to touch me. She was flaunting herself in front of my list so that I was unable to focus on our plan for the day.

I had assumed that sex was out of the question this morning because I had been virtually gone for three days. I know that Pam needs lots of quality time together to be in the mood, and lately we'd had anything but quality time. I was enjoying this attention, and was secretly wishing this could happen every day, but I was puzzled by the sudden rush of enthusiasm on Pam's part.

Eventually I stopped trying to be task oriented and asked her, "What's up with all this attention? Don't get me wrong, I love it! But I don't understand why you are so excited when we haven't spent time together."

She looked me in the eyes with my favorite sensuous gaze and said, "You wish you were independently wealthy and could love me all day long."

The anticipation that had been building in her heart for the last three days led to one of the best memories I have of the potential of intimate love. I learned that day that building anticipation is one of the most powerful aspects of romance!

Unconditional Love

ED YOUNG

 know of a couple who have been married over fifty years. They have three grown children and two grandchildren. He is a retired civil servant, in excellent health, who loves to golf and plays as often as he can. She suffers from Parkinson's disease and her condition deteriorates almost daily. A few years ago she suffered a stroke that has altered her personality and limited her physical capabilities, causing her to require constant care and supervision. In appearance and in nature she has changed greatly from the wife she once was.

Last Thanksgiving this couple ate dinner at their daughter's home. He helped her with her food, as he has for some time. After dinner the table was cleared for coffee and dessert. When her pie was served, she immediately—to her daughter's alarm—turned it off her plate and onto the table, and tried to eat it. He calmly brushed aside their attempts to clean up the mess; instead he slid his own dessert onto the table as well, smiled, patted her hand reassuringly, and topped both his dessert and hers with a big dollop of whipped cream!

It is easy to know the real thing when you see it, isn't it?

Freckle-Faced Beauty

NANCY GODBEHERE

The youngest of our children, Holly, was a little cutie towhead with big China blue eyes, fair skin, and lots of freckles. Her sister, Sally, who was three years older, was another beauty with chestnut brown hair, big brown eyes, and a creamy olive skin. Holly longed to have the flawless, freckle-less complexion like her sister. As cute and sweet as Holly was, her freckles started to become a big problem for her. She hated those freckles, complaining about them almost every day. "Momma, I'll never be pretty like Sally as long as I have those freckles."

Even our pastor had to be gently reminded not to call her "freckle face" at church because then she cried all the way home. She seemed so unhappy—even angry. *Can a six-year-old be depressed?* I wondered. *This is ridiculous. We can't seem to convince her that her freckles are not important to who she really is. Why can't she understand how special she is to us?*

I didn't know what to do. I couldn't get rid of her freckles and it was getting to be a huge problem. Her school work started to suffer and her teacher suggested a tutor to help her in reading. I prayed every day, "God, please, help Holly feel good about herself."

Within two weeks, we received a letter in the mail from a modeling agency that wanted Holly for modeling. We read the letter to her and she felt very special—actually good about herself.

She smiled, "I guess my freckles aren't so bad after all. It's a shame Sally can't have freckles."

Two days later, Holly came home from school announcing she had won the United Way Poster Contest for her grade and would be a special guest of honor at a downtown restaurant. Her father and I would be her guests. She actually beamed with pride.

God provided abundant answers to my prayers and Holly was once again our happy little towhead with beautiful China blue eyes and a light sprinkling of cute little freckles.

"When You Least Expect It"

PATTY STUMP

he meeting room emptied, yet a young mom and I savored the rare opportunity to simply sit and chat. She cheerfully shared of the current events in her life, yet fought back tears when our conversation turned to her son.

She said with pain in her eyes, "He had so much going for him. He was athletic, energetic, an excellent football player. Now he's on the sidelines, unable to engage in contact sports due to an eye impairment. I feel so bad for him. I wish I could do something. He doesn't seem to mind being on the sidelines. He's taking it all in stride. But as his Mom, I want to fix it, to make his life all it is supposed to be. He had so much going for him."

"What if . . . what if this isn't 'Plan B?'" I responded. "What if these circumstances are actually part of what God would consider 'Plan A' for your son's life?"

"'Plan A'? You mean, these circumstances could be something God is using in His overall plan for my son's life? Not an error in the way things are supposed to work out?"

"That's right. How would you feel about things then?" I asked.

"Hmmm. . . . 'Plan A'. That would change everything," she replied. "If these circumstances are being used to further God's plan, then he's not going to miss out on anything God has in store for him. I'd never looked at it that way before."

"Well, give it some thought. It's late and we both need to get some rest, but before you go to bed, let me say a quick prayer to end our time together." We bowed our heads and I continued. "Thank You, Lord, for this family and their love for one another. And thank You for the plans You have in store for this young fella. How comforting it is to know that all things do indeed work together for the good."

I was confident the Lord hadn't forgotten her son, and that He had a plan for his life that would unfold just as God planned. Undoubtedly his future activities would be different than what he and his parents had anticipated, but it didn't mean that he would merely exist on the 'sidelines' of life, With that thought in mind, we ended our conversation.

The next morning our paths crossed briefly as we both resumed the hurried pace that life so often brings. She paused long enough to give me a brief hug and whispered quietly, "Thank you for the insights you passed along. After our visit, I spent some time thinking about my son's struggles as being 'Plan A' rather than a detour from God's plans. God has already used that perspective to change my outlook and encourage my heart. I can't wait to see how His plans for our son unfold. Thank you."

I passed her thank you on to God, not only for giving me timely words and insights, but also for reminding *me* to rest in the fact that He will accomplish in and through me what He desires.

Cookie Drops

MARIE ASNER

ast Christmas, an unexpected package arrived in the mail. It was from a childhood friend who lived 600 miles from me, nicknamed "Cookie." She would joke, "We have known each other since I was two and you were three, living at opposite ends of the block." Cookie met her husband at my wedding and they were married a year later. We kept in touch through the years—a phone call for a birthday, postcards during vacation. Somehow, though, I always knew where she was.

Five years ago, my aunt unexpectedly called me to say Cookie's mother died. I phoned my friend's home only to have her children say they didn't know where Mom was. I knew. Her mother's phone number—even after thirty years, came to mind, and I dialed the number. Cookie answered. It was as though thirty years were wiped away and we were teens again. She said, "How did you know where to find me?" I always knew where she was—an inner connection that never diminished through the years.

When that package arrived from her that Christmas, I opened it to find a pair of crystal earrings and recognized the pattern as coming from a necklace belonging to her mother. My friend decided to have the old necklace taken apart and earrings made for her daughters and a pair for me. What a treasured moment this was, as I tried them on and remembered the occasions I had seen the necklace.

Several months later, my friend called to say she was about to have cancer surgery and the prognosis was not good. Before I could drive the distance, the Lord took her home. The news was devastating and I moved, fog-bound, through the next weeks. My friend didn't realize she was saying "good-bye" when she took the necklace apart. We were receiving parts of her life to remind us of her, but no one knew it at the time.

I took the earrings to my jeweler to have the backs secured. As he gently lifted them from the box, he said, "Oh, these are drops." Yes, they are—"Cookie" drops—and I know where she is. I can find her anytime in my heart.

Abundant Encouragement

RICHARD KENNEDY

ne Sunday evening, I was to give my very first sermon—at my home church's worship service no less! I was eighteen years old and scared to death. I was sure God had called me to ministry, but not so sure about a preaching ministry.

I failed miserably at an opening joke and went on to tell them everything I knew—and it lasted seven minutes. Seven minutes! Sermons were supposed to last 30 to 40 minutes in my church. In a panic, all I knew to do was dismiss in prayer.

While someone else closed the service, I ducked into a side room off to the side of the platform. It was also customary in our church that the pastor or guest preacher slip out during closing prayer to the back of the church and shake hands with people as they left. But there was no way I was going to face those people!

My home church pastor, Charles Harris, could see the pain in my face. He followed me into the side room. "Let's go greet the people," he said.

"No, I can't," I replied, my eyes filled with shame. "Please go and apologize for me."

Then he spoke a few brief words of encouragement to me that I have never forgotten. "Preaching is a calling, but it's also a skill that takes times to develop. Now come out with me and let the people love you."

We stood shoulder to shoulder as we greeted the congregation and one by one they told me how good my message was. I knew they were used to better, but I let the people love me, and that was thirty years ago. Since then, God has privileged me with a dynamic preaching ministry that wouldn't have occurred if that wise pastor hadn't encouraged me to let others love me.

An Operation of the Heart

ANESA CRONIN

bout nine years ago I underwent an appendectomy. However, because poisons had entered my blood system, within a few short days my health rapidly failed. When the doctor saw me, he immediately arranged for a second operation. Upon my admission to the hospital, at 9:30 that night, the staff virtually ran my gurney to the operating room.

Though I was only in my mid-thirties and had much going for myself, I was secretly hoping that I wouldn't make it through the surgery. It's hard to admit, but I hoped the Lord would take me home. Despite my active Christian walk and commitments, I was very weary of being single and missing out on having my own family.

When I "came to" in recovery and heard the nurse whisper, "You're very lucky to be alive," my heart virtually sank. I was utterly disappointed to be alive.

In the next few days, I began receiving a barrage of gifts and flowers. Friends circled my bed almost every evening, bringing me laughter and joy. The nurses stated they had never seen anything like it. When the flower courier headed toward their station, they would just redirect him to my room with a point of the finger.

Though I did not have a mate or children of my own, God made it clear to me that He had abundantly blessed me with true friends and good family. I had new purpose because of the awesome responsibility He'd given me to nurture those relationships, lend them encouragement, and reciprocate their love. God mended not only my incisions, but my attitude as well. He replaced my self-pity with gratitude.

Since the recovery of both my body and my spirit, souls have been won for Christ, many homeless people have received a meal, missionaries have been supported, friends' marriages have been reconciled, and rebellious teens have been corrected because of my ministry-related activities, job experiences, and personal choices.

I remember a preacher once saying, "We're in the kingdom now and are just heaven bound." So what was my rush? Christ will return at the right time. And He will receive me in due time. Though heaven will undoubtedly be better than earth, right now, sharing God's love with others is abundant reward and purpose for living.

Blanket Tents and Yesterday

DORIS HAYS NORTHSTROM

 heard giggling in the hall as a note flew under the bathroom door and hit the tub. With stories read and prayers said, my children were tucked in for the night. As I picked up the paper, three distinct knocks echoed on the wall between the bathroom and the children's bedroom. I knocked back three times, and then read the scrawled note splendidly decorated with cursive circle lace and a stick figure in a wide skirt with wild, wiry hair and a large pink heart. "Dear momma, thanks for the raisin cookies. You are the best mom. Can we make blanket tents over the clothesline tomorrow and have a circus?"

Those young years passed so swiftly and the children grew into their teens, still lighting life with surprises. As everyone settled in for the evening, I would slip into that safe place in the bathtub where mothers relax at the end of a day. Deep in thought, for a moment I was startled by three deliberate, though familiar, knocks on the bathroom wall.

The children remembered—and so did I. It was our signal, homegrown from childhood days, that said, "It's good to be here together. I know you're there and I love you." Through storms or sunshine, those knocks reminded us that we were family, we had each other, and we were strong.

More years slipped away in the winds of brown-bag lunches with notes tucked inside, backyard ballgames, and valentines. The children grew up and moved into homes and apartments of their own.

After a long struggle, I had to tell them, "Your father and I are divorcing." Our home sold the week it went on the market. Gone were 38 years of cooking omelets, lighting birthday candles, and sleeping on the deck under the stars. Two of the four children had been there since birth. In two months someone else would be planting daffodil bulbs and deciding where to put their Christmas tree.

We walked through the motions of packing and giving things away—furniture, tools, yard equipment, and wood piled by the shed ready for the next two winters. But all that wood couldn't keep us warm in that house any longer. The children drove up in their trucks and hauled the piles of fir and alder to their homes.

That last night, before new owners moved in, I waved the older children and their families off toward their homes, then finished scrubbing the sink and tub in my rose-papered bathroom. Terri and Brian sorted through the last of their stored record albums and tapes. I prayed through a mist of memories, "Lord, this is the toughest night in this family's history. All those years in Your presence and prayer have strengthened me, but my heart feels deep sadness for my children. Help us to make it through to a new day."

Suddenly, three distinct knocks on the wall vibrated in the emptiness of the house. I took a deep breath, dropped my cleaning sponge, and knocked back from my side of the wall. I ran in to hug my son. His eyes glistened, looking sad, yet he squared his shoulders, and my daughter put arms around both of us in a bear hug.

No bedtime prayers, blanket tents, or homegrown circus clowns like in the young days, but my children were letting me know we were family, we had God, we were strong.

Finally, I boxed up my cleaning supplies and remembered the stick-figure momma with the wiry hair and large laced heart on the pages of a long ago note. I turned out all the lights, firmly gripped the front door knob, pulling it shut. Listening carefully in the stillness of dusk closing in, I could hear the laughter and the wonder of us all, way back then. I knocked three times and smiled.

City Camper

SANDRA PALMER CARR

s I pulled into the parking lot on my way to get a haircut, I saw her. Disheveled and dirty, she was old, her skin tanned and weather-beaten. Her gray hair matted, she sat on the curb, her mouth drawn inward against her gums. The rusted shopping cart beside her was loaded with goods, tied down like a covered wagon. She looked at me as I drove by.

"Dear God," I said aloud, "How can she eat the food she needs without any teeth?"

A still, small voice whispered: "Get her something to eat." I wondered what she could chew that would give her strength.

The supermarket was a startling contrast as well-dressed shoppers busily came and went. I roamed the pastry aisle and found some cinnamon rolls. Milk seemed the next obvious choice. Then a further nudging in my spirit prompted me to select some small cans of apple juice. It was mid-morning and breakfast made sense. But what if she's hungry for lunch? I grabbed a roast beef sandwich from the deli section. Hurriedly I got into the express line, which seemed slower than ever.

"Please, Lord, don't let her get away from me."

By the time I returned and looked along the row of small businesses where she had been resting, I couldn't find her. She was gone.

"Lord, You told me to get her something to eat. Help me find her."

I got back into the car, worried the food would be wasted if I couldn't give it away. I prayed again. Entering one busy street, turning right onto another, my eyes scanned the sidewalks. "She must be close, Lord, but where?"

Returning to the shopping center, I spotted her. She was camped a few feet outside the entrance to Denny's Restaurant. I parked again. When I approached the cart, she wasn't there. I thought she might be using the restroom.

Then they emerged, laughing and talking. A restaurant employee who seemed to know the homeless woman gave her a sack. Almost simultaneously, I offered mine. "God doesn't want you begging for food today," I said, hearing the piety in my own voice. The other woman commented about the items she had given her, thanked me, and quickly returned to the restaurant.

Introducing myself, I asked, "What's your name?"

"Ruth," she said, and smiled, revealing a mouthful of grayish, yellow dentures. God's wisdom that had directed my roast beef selection was confirmed.

Ruth continued talking as if we'd been visiting for awhile. Then she said, "I'm 85 years old, and I've never had to beg God for anything. God always provides." Pointing to the two sacks, she said, "This is so much. If it's too much, I'll have food to share with someone else."

We hugged. She smelled fresh and clean. Then I asked her, "Do you know the Lord Jesus?"

"Oh, yes." She patted a small brown Bible on the top of the mound in the shopping cart. It was very worn with papers and cards tucked between the pages.

Ruth asked me where I went to church. I told her, then added, "And if you're ever over that way, stop in. We'd love to have you." I smiled to myself, knowing that she truly would be welcome where I worship.

She credited the Holy Spirit with our meeting. I agreed. We shared a prayer.

"The nights are the hardest," she said, "'cause I'm out there and things happen. One night two young men were waiting around a corner. I put my hands straight up in the air and yelled, 'Help me, Jesus!' And they ran away."

Ruth laughed. "The Lord takes care of me."

We hugged again, and offered the Lord's blessings to one another. She mentioned we'd see each other in Heaven.

I got into my car and cried.

"Forgive me, Lord, for being so prideful—always thinking I'm the giver of Your gifts. Today You gave me Ruth, a dear, sweet lesson in humility. You are so good."

Yes, Ruth was right. God always provides abundantly. And if it's too much, we can share with someone else.

"Mom, I'm Leaving Home!"

JOAN CLAYTON

rom the moment they brought him to me in the hospital, I knew this little precious cherub was a gift from God. Lane looked like an angel. His daddy stood by the nursery window for hours, just looking at him. Everyone that passed by heard: "That's my boy!" Lane loved to be cuddled. He hardly ever fretted. All he needed was a dry diaper, a bottle, a little loving, and then off to sleep again.

All too soon Lane became a toddler. My husband, Emmitt, came home for lunch every day just to hold and play with him. Emmitt and I sat opposite each other and held our arms toward him. He toddled back and forth, literally falling into our arms, laughing and cooing.

In first grade, Lane came home one day and said, "Mommie, I thought fleas were brown."

"They are," I responded.

"But my music teacher taught us a song that said Mary had a little lamb. Its fleas were white as snow!"

Lane was older than most of the other children on our block, but the neighbors always wanted Lane to play in their yard. He had such patience and was so kind to the little ones.

Lane wanted to be baptized at a young age. His heart was very tender and we didn't want to discourage him in any way from making the most important decision of his life. After talking with him at length, making sure he understood the commitment, we agreed.

In junior high, Lane came home one day and said, "Mom, I guess I have a girl friend. Louise told me I was her boy friend, does that make it so? Oh, I want to be a friend, but I don't know about this girl stuff."

Lane went to high school with great promise. He had already won many awards, and he excelled in all of his sophomore classes. We had begun to make plans for a Christian college after his senior year.

And then it happened! The world came crashing down around me! Completely out of the blue, at sixteen years old, Lane came home from school one day and emptied his closet. He put all of his clothes in his red Monte Carlo and informed us that he was moving four hundred miles away. He was quitting school to work in a friend's dad's ice house.

To say we were in shock is to put it mildly! It was like I was watching a heartbreaking movie. *This is happening to someone else, not me!*

Emmitt was just as shocked. He asked, "Is this some kind of a joke? You surely aren't serious!"

But Lane was serious. Emmitt tried to reason with him in every possible way. He reminded him of the great future he had ahead of him and the possibility of scholarships for college.

I looked at Lane in total disbelief. *This can't be Lane. How can a teenager turn into a completely different person overnight? I don't even know my own child.*

Emmitt and I pleaded for hours. It was early April, and even though the days were getting longer, shadows were creeping over our yard and into our hearts. My mind flashed back to Lane's boyhood bedtime prayers: "Jesus, thank You that my Mommie and Daddy love me!" My heart was literally tearing in two.

Lane was determined to leave. What could we do? Take away his keys? Try to ground him? Forbid him to leave?

"Please, don't go!" I cried repeatedly. I held on to him. Lane pulled away from me as if I were a stranger. I ached all over.

Emmitt's face was pale and drawn. He took Lane in his arms and told him how much we loved him and that we would never stop praying for him. Emmitt then looked at me through tears and said in a broken voice, "We can't keep him a prisoner. We have to let him go and trust God to bring him back."

"We can't do that!" I screamed. "He's only sixteen!"

"We have invested love, truth, and prayer in him. Now we must put him in God's hands." Emmitt's eyes were full of pain and it pierced my soul to see the hurt.

We clung to Lane and prayed. Our tears fell on his feet. We watched him drive away as far as we could see.

Emmitt slept restlessly that night. I couldn't sleep at all. The clock struck midnight. Then 1 o'clock. 2 o'clock. 3 o'clock. 4 o'clock.

At 4:30, I thought I heard a car pull up in our driveway. Could it possibly be? "Dear God, please let it be."

I ran to the front door. I recognized the loud sound of the exhaust pipes on Lane's car. It was Lane!

"Emmitt, it's Lane! He's come back! Thank You, Jesus, Lane's come home!"

Emmitt came racing to the door. He grabbed Lane in a great big bear hug. Our hearts were overflowing with gratitude.

Lane hugged him back. He swept me off my feet. Even though he wouldn't admit it, I think he was every bit as happy to be back as we were to have him back. Lane's words are engraved in my memory:

"It didn't work out! The farther down the road I got, the more I realized how I would miss those Saturday night enchiladas and Sunday hot rolls. No one can cook like you, Mom! But most of all, I found out I could leave home, but I could not leave love."

She Dances Now

LETTIE J. KIRKPATRICK

e received the news on January 15th—Shela's first birthday. "Your daughter has a terminal muscle disease. She will never walk or gain strength. She will, instead, progressively weaken until the wasting is fatal. She has six months to a year to live."

We were hearing, in shocked disbelief, the first of many pronouncements that would be voiced to us by Shela's doctors in hospital waiting rooms. While the estimated life expectancy was very erroneous, the disease did all the other predicted damage. It destroyed Shela's ability to sit alone and care for most of her personal needs, limiting her to only the lightest of tasks. She could not even turn herself at night. It also created respiratory and skeletal weakness. This resulted in frequent pneumonia and the need for a spinal fusion when she was seven.

At age twelve, Shela's first year of junior high, Shela crashed in her wheelchair off a steep sidewalk at school. Her head received the force of the blow when the 100-pound chair slammed her into the asphalt. After performing emergency brain surgery, the neurosurgeon in Pediatric Intensive Care told us, "Part of her brain was pulverized—I had to remove a portion of the left hemisphere. The prognosis is grim. If she survives, we don't know what the results of this surgery will be."

We were stunned and numb. Would God really deprive this spunky, joyful little girl of her only apparent asset? Her mental capabilities were all that remained untouched by the ravages of her muscle disorder.

But through prayer, God's grace, and excellent care, Shela rallied. She defeated brain swelling, pneumonia, and respirator dependency to return home three weeks later. Although she lost more of her little remaining physical strength, her mind was intact. This same doctor wrote in her hospital record, "This child miraculously survived. I am exceedingly well pleased." Her recovery was so complete that she graduated from high school six years later wearing the white robe that designated her an Honors Student. She was awarded an academic scholarship to attend college.

However, following a successful year of college, at age nineteen, Shela's journey of physical struggle came to its close. Our moments of waiting were completed with a final, painful declaration. The internist, who one hour earlier had successfully implanted a permanent feeding tube to compensate for Shela's decreased swallowing strength, made a second call to our waiting area. His first report had informed us that all was well. Shela was talking and smiling and would soon be returning to her room. After a puzzling delay, he called with words now branded on my heart. "Your daughter has gone into cardiac arrest. We are working with her in a life-threatening situation."

Despite diligent efforts to save her life, Shela went home to be with Jesus July 28, 1993.

But these hospital dramas only tell part of Shela's story. Those of us who had the great privilege of "walking" with her will be forever changed by her presence among us. That number includes her dad and I, her four younger brothers, our church family, other family members, and many friends. She was a model of courage and contentment in the face of life's limitations. Although not a candidate for sainthood, she delighted in experiencing life vicariously through the joy of others.

Perhaps her favorite outing was to the public dance recitals of one of her younger friends. She loved watching this bubbly seven-year-old display her skills at tap and jazz to a mall full of onlookers. Shela herself seemed transported as Ambra moved to the rhythm of the music. Ambra's mom once said to me, "Shela had the heart of a dancer." One of my most precious possessions is an ornament given to me the Christmas following Shela's death. It is a lovely ballerina angel.

I believe now that Shela had a premonition of her approaching death. She kept personal journals that are filled with prayers. She recorded the joy of experiencing everyday events such as a movie or a trip out to eat. She never failed to thank God for her health! But the summer of her home-going she had underlined and discussed a verse in Isaiah that intrigued her. Isaiah 57:1, 2 states, "The righteous man perishes and no man takes it to heart; And devout men are taken away while no one understands. For the righteous man is taken away from evil, He enters into peace." (NASB)

Shela also asked me as we prepared for her final trip to the hospital, "Mama, if I die, will you remember me?" I responded to this unbelievable question at her memorial service with a written piece called "A Mother's Tribute." I detailed the incredible impact of her life on mine.

As I strive to grasp the reality that the seemingly endless struggles of those years are over for us both, I take great comfort in knowing we fought a good fight. And in moments when the pain of loss overwhelms me, I remember my ballerina angel and God's assurance in Ecclesiastes 3:4 that "there is a time to mourn, and a time to dance."

Shela dances now!

A Precious Jewell

NANCY E. PETERSON

I took care of Mom in our home for as long as I was able. She has rheumatoid arthritis, fibromyalgia, and severe depression. Evidently it was the combination of medication that caused her confusion. It got steadily worse and she started falling frequently. I have a bad back from an old break and a genetic heart condition. I tried to get her up on my own, but the day finally came when it was beyond me. She fell against the closed door in the bathroom, wedging it into the jam, at eleven at night. My husband was at work and our son was still very young. The only thing I could think to do was call the paramedics.

A neighbor babysat while I drove to the hospital behind the ambulance. Nothing was broken, but we were told to take her to our doctor the next day. He suggested we put her in a skilled nursing facility and signed the papers; but, bless her, Mom had already been telling me she needed to be in one. Within five days she was a resident at what we now call "The Home."

Five years later I look back on her history at "The Home" and realize she has taught me many lessons about making lemonade when life gives you lemons. Most of the residents who are put in skilled nursing facilities are angry. They feel abandoned and as if everyone is just waiting for them to die. Some I've even heard say, "I wish I'd die and get it over with." Not Mom.

Mom's in a lot of pain. She has also had both hips replaced and gall bladder surgery since she moved there, yet she visits with the other patients, bringing them a warm smile and sometimes even a hug. She even "visits" with the ones who make no sense or can't talk because she feels they might be lonely. She has gotten to know the staff and asks how their families are. Pictures of their children hang on her bulletin board.

As I push her down the hall in her wheel chair, she'll stop me so she can visit with someone who has Alzheimer's or a stroke victim who is particularly out of it. Yet somehow they know it's Jewell and they smile for her.

When we're both up to it, we get in the car, and go park under a pepper tree to visit. She tells me about her Bible studies and what she has learned from God since our last visit. She also shares about the other patients; who's doing a little better or a little worse, and who's passed on, hopefully to be with God. She tries to tell others about the Lord, when they're willing to listen.

She still wants to know about the lives of my family and my brother. Her wisdom is delivered with love.

Sometimes I get to feeling sorry for myself when I can't keep up with my family and friends because of my own health problems. I'm tempted to pout, cry, or even lash out at the world. Then I remember Mom's bright smile and generous heart in spite of her ill health and living in "The Home." She's teaching me to tap into God's strength and love when things get difficult. He *never* lets us down.

Ben's Real Grandma

HELEN LUECKE

doption!" I said, shaking my head at Richard, my husband. "Why would Kirk and Cathy want to adopt a baby when they have Patrick? One grandson is fine with me."

Richard looked up from his newspaper and frowned. "Stay out of it, Grandma Cozy. You know their chances of having another baby are slim."

The statement was true. After Patrick's birth, our son and daughter-in-law had tried to conceive for almost three years. They had gone to specialists and had many tests. They were told to go home and wait.

Later that night, unable to sleep, I mulled over the adoption issue. Would I be able to love a baby who didn't have a single Luecke family gene? Would I be partial to Patrick? I could not answer.

As I tossed, one word pounded in my mind: adoption. Finally I became so exhausted, I fell asleep.

About six months later Kirk called with the news. "We're getting a baby, Mom. He's due in two months. It's going to be an open adoption."

I felt a twinge of fear. What did open adoption mean? How long did it take before the adoption became final?

Early one March morning, the telephone rang. "Mom, Dad!" Kirk almost shouted, "Ben's here. We have our baby."

The following month Richard and I drove to our son's home in Dallas to meet Ben. As I held him, I studied his features: big blue eyes, not much hair, and a cute little nose. *Just like any other baby*, I thought. An emptiness settled in my chest as I handed him back to Kirk. Then I raced outside with Patrick to watch him ride his bike.

One evening after we returned home, I watched a TV program about adopted children. I stared in horror as a mother reclaimed her daughter from a couple who had adopted her several years before.

How cruel, I thought. I began to sob and chills covered my body. "Could they do that to Ben?" I asked Richard.

He held me close for a minute and said, "I suppose they could. We'll just have to wait and see."

Later that night, I prayed for Ben, Kirk, and Cathy, and the birth parents, but peace did not come. *Don't get too attached to Ben,* I told myself.

The next morning I telephoned Kirk. "Did Ben's birth father sign the adoption papers? Is his mother still going through with the adoption?"

"Mom, you watched that TV program, didn't you?"

"Yes."

"Stop worrying. Ben is ours. His father signed the papers. His mother isn't going to change her mind."

During the six-month waiting period, my stomach stayed tied in knots. When the adoption became final, I relaxed a little.

One day my sister Sandra and I indulged in our favorite pastime, exchanging grandbaby stories.

"All you ever talk about is Patrick," Sandra said. "You do have another grandson, and soon he'll be old enough to notice the difference."

I hadn't deceived Sandra about my fears.

"I'm not partial to Patrick," I snapped. "Every time I buy Patrick a gift, I get one for Ben."

"Yeah, you do, but I'm not talking about gifts. I'm talking about love. Think about it, Helen."

In February, Kirk telephoned, "Mom, next month, we're taking the church youth group skiing in Colorado. Would you keep Ben for a week?"

"Sure," I replied, though I wasn't sure at all.

The week before the ski trip, I talked to God often. "Lord, You know my heart, and You know how I've acted the last two years. Help me to accept Ben as my own flesh. I place this concern in Your hands."

The day Ben arrived he made himself at home. The blue-eyed, brown-haired two-year-old found the toy box and scattered small cars, blocks, books, and crayons all over the room.

The following days, each morning at 5 a.m., Ben's usual getting-up time, we watched Barney and Winnie the Pooh videos. Later we walked to the park. Still the fears remained, knotted in my chest. I refused to let go.

The night before Ben went home, after I gave him his bath, we played "this little piggy went to market." I rubbed lotion on his feet and legs and listened to his deep laughter echo through the house. I grabbed each toe and kissed his squirming feet. Next he marched behind me as we went to tell Grampy good night.

Back in the bedroom, Ben pointed to the rocking chair. I sat down and he climbed onto my lap. "I love you, Ben," I said kissing his pug nose.

"Love, night-night," he answered giving me a soggy kiss. I savored the moment of baby innocence and marveled at his complete trust in me. Ben's warm body, snuggled on my shoulder, felt exactly right. I breathed in the fresh fragrance of baby powder and lotion and continued to rock.

There in the stillness, words written by Pearl Buck that I had read long ago floated through my mind: "Love cannot be forced, love cannot be coaxed and teased. It comes out of Heaven, unasked and unsought."

A tear rolled down my cheek as I realized that God had given me the privilege of being Ben's grandma for the remainder of my life. I tried to look into the future. What would Ben be when he grew up? Would he trust in God? Suddenly I knew that with all my heart I wanted to be part of Ben's life.

I hugged him close and whispered near his ear, "I love you, Ben." This time the words were true. At last, I had that special abundant feeling for Ben—the grandma feeling. Whatever was ahead, I would always be Ben's *real* grandma.

A Child of God

RONICA STROMBERG

was pregnant with our second child, eagerly anticipating what God had in store for us, when my obstetrician telephoned me unexpectedly.

"I've received the results of your blood test," he said gravely, "and it indicates that the child you're carrying may have Down's Syndrome."

"Oh," I said, stunned. "Okay."

The other end of the telephone line was silent for a few moments. Finally, the doctor asked, "Do you know what Down's Syndrome is?"

"Yes," I said. I had grown up almost next door to a girl with Down's Syndrome. Although none of the children in the neighborhood had played often with her, no one had teased her or picked on her either. She had seemed content riding her bicycle around the block each day, a Barbie doll strapped to the handlebars for company.

Once, I had asked the girl's younger sister, "What is it like having her for a sister?"

"My mom says we're a special family," she had answered. "God doesn't pick many families to give a child with Down's Syndrome to, so He must have thought we had lots of love to give."

And they had, as I remembered.

Now as the doctor rattled on about further tests, genetic counseling, and the possibility of terminating the pregnancy, I found myself interrupting with a firm no. "I want this baby," I said. "I think kids with Down's Syndrome are great."

The doctor was silent again. No doubt he was thinking of the difficulty of raising a child with Down's Syndrome—the tremendous amount of patience and love required—and questioning how much thought I had given to my decision.

I had my own doubts that I was up to the task. And yet, I knew that God knew what He was doing even if I did not. In Exodus 4:11, He says, "Who gave man his mouth? Who makes him deaf or mute? Who gives him sight or makes him blind? Is it not I, the Lord?" God had plans for this child I was carrying.

I already held the answer I would give my first child if he came to me asking why I chose to give birth to a child with Down's Syndrome: "Because we're a special family. God doesn't pick many families to give a child with Down's Syndrome to, so he must have thought we had abundant love to give."

God's Healing Love

RUTH E. MCDANIEL

hen I was a child, I often watched with an aching
hunger as other mothers lovingly touched their
children. My mother was raised in a harsh, unemo-
tional household. Displays of affection were non-
existent. I was never cuddled or felt the joy of being rocked while
my mother sang a soothing hymn.

I was determined to shower my own children with love and
affection, so I did. Nearly every chair in my house rocks, and I
sang to my three sons until they were old enough to leave home!

Along the way, I began to share small hugs and kisses with my
parents and siblings. At first, it was stiff and awkward, but it was
never rejected. And, now, an affectionate exchange is not only
accepted, it's expected! What a difference a loving touch makes!

Through the years, I've enlarged my circle of "hug-recipients"
to include friends. Once again, no one appears to be offended.
Just the opposite, in fact, people seem delighted!

Last year, I began to volunteer at a nursing home. Can you
guess what my primary duties are? I'm the official "hug" distribu-
tor! Everyone responds to a show of affection. The more love
you give, the more you receive. My cup truly overflows.

My most gratifying moment came from one of the residents of
the nursing home, a dementia patient. These patients are often
hostile and Regina's illness was advanced. She spent her days
storming through the halls ranting unintelligibly. Most people
stayed away from her, not wanting to suffer her wrath and unexpected blows. I watched her from a distance for weeks. Then,
one sunny, spring day, I decided to join her as she marched an-
grily around the outside of the building.

At first, Regina yelled at me and raised her fists, threaten-
ingly. But I kept pace and continued to chatter about the green
grass and the lovely flowers. At one point, I said, "Regina, isn't
God's world beautiful?" She stopped in mid-stride and stared at
me. Suddenly, she gave me a big smile! A feeling of warmth and

love flowed through me and I asked, "Can I hug you?" She nodded and we embraced, heartily. We finished our walk, arm-in-arm,
while I shared God's Word with her. Since that day, whenever
Regina sees me, she holds out her arms for her weekly hug and
affirmation: "God loves you and so do I!" Her healing is a great
witness to everyone at the nursing home of the abundant power
of God's love and hugs!

Provision of Love

ALENA STUTSMAN

e were going to be married! Could it be that at the age of forty-two, I had discovered my love at last? In September, 1972, I was in my ninth year of teaching Christian school in Washington, when at Christmas time, Skip, a widower with seven children, came into my life. Needless to say, lonesomeness and boredom melted like winter snow. As spring came, friendship blossomed into love.

One evening as we munched fish and chips in a Safeway parking lot, Skip and I seriously discussed God's will for us. We compared Scriptures and our thoughts. All Skip's well-laid plans fled as he had intended to propose the following Saturday on a romantic trip to Port Townsend. Now the time seemed just right and he did it! I accepted and knew that the truth of Psalm 68:6—"God setteth the solitary in families" (KJV)—was actually going to be a reality for me.

Then began the thrilling days of preparing for our wedding. My teaching salary and savings were inadequate for wedding expenses, but God provided. The mother of one of my students popped into my classroom. Beaming, she exclaimed, "I've been waiting forever to ask you if you'd like to wear my wedding dress?" When I slipped into the lovely lace-over-satin dress, it fit like a dream. A friend dry-cleaned it at a shop where she worked and another lent me her beautiful veil.

But the wedding expenses were numerous. Skip's daughters, Virginia and Elizabeth, would need new dresses as the candle lighters, and Esther would receive gifts from the guests. She wanted something new, too. Imagine my gratefulness when a family friend gave me money to purchase dress fabric. I asked another friend to make the dresses. When I picked up the beautiful pink and green gowns, she said, "This is my wedding gift."

I wanted my mother to share in the nuptial preparations and get to know Skip and his family. When I became engaged, she had expressed concern. "You know you're not very strong, Alena," she said. "Do you think you can handle being the mother of a large family?" How special it was to have her come for the entire month of July and see how I could handle such busy activity! Mom accompanied me when I ordered the reception napkins and purchased my going-away dress. A fellow teacher and her daughters baked cookies for the reception with Mom's help. When we applied for our marriage license, we had only five minutes to spare. Mom ran breathlessly up the hill with us to the courthouse.

She traveled with me to Pacific Beach to see a friend. We stopped in Montsano to shop. I had searched for opaque cloth for curtains for Skip's forest-green Ford station wagon. Miraculously, we found flowered multi-colored matching fabric. Mom did most of the sewing and soon the project was done.

The blessings continued. Women from both our churches and my school hosted wedding showers. My fourth grade class surprised me with a shower, as did my Pioneer Girls' group. A family friend baked the beautiful wedding cake for half-price.

One of my students persuaded her mom to get flowers for my wedding while they were in Hawaii. The local florist arranged the antherium in the altar bouquets. Providentially, Skip worked there as a carpenter, resulting in a twenty per-cent discount on the wedding floral package. One evening he remarked, "Guess what, even though I'm not a regular employee, I'm getting a week's paid vacation! Now we can easily go for two weeks on our wedding trip."

Innumerable other things were needed and always God supplied the money or the support. Friends, Paul and Florence Turnidge, where I lived, graciously allowed Mom to occupy one of their bedrooms and Florence hosted our rehearsal dinner and included my family from Wisconsin.

A crucial thing happened on August 3, 1973, the day of our wedding. My sister, Ruth, was pressing her bridesmaid dress. The iron was too hot and took its shape out of the front waist. She screamed and began sobbing. Everyone came to the rescue and sister Ardy made the alteration.

A student's parents were hairdressers and checked the coiffures of all the ladies in the wedding party. Besides the professional photographer, a dear friend took casual pictures and arranged an album for us.

Because the huge crowd took longer to seat, the wedding was twenty minutes late. Skip was greatly relieved when someone came to get him in the church basement. He wondered if I was "backing out" on him.

The beautiful candlelight wedding proceeded without further problems. The double-ring ceremony climaxed with each of the children handing me a red rose, even three-year-old Arnold, who had to be awakened! It was a very moving experience, and many guests shed tears of joy.

God also wondrously provided for our honeymoon. It was important to have the right person stay with our children. We could not have had a more caring, dependable lady than we had chosen.

Our honeymoon suite for three nights was a riverside cabin near Index, Washington, a gift of a former pastor and his wife. Then we drove leisurely to Astoria, Oregon, and down the coast. We enjoyed Crater Lake and the trip back through eastern Oregon.

When we arrived home, we opened wedding gifts from nearly four hundred guests. We were rich in wonderful friends and relatives!

I could never doubt that God had guided Skip and me together. Years in His care have rolled by. Now twenty-five years later, I can say, "God is still an abundant provider."

The Flag

TERESA GRIGGS

t had been almost three years since my daughter, Mallory, was called from this earth and went on to be with the Lord. I missed her every day, but on holidays her absence was so much more painful. Mallory loved holidays as most children do. The Fourth of July was one of her very favorites. We live in a small town which still celebrates with a huge fireworks display held at the end of the day. Our family, grandparents, aunts, uncles, and friends all gather at a certain spot to enjoy the festivities.

As the Fourth approached this year, and I began to make plans for our family, I really felt it would just be too difficult for me to go to the fireworks show that evening, even though my sons would probably protest. I could see in my mind Mallory's glowing face admiring the fantastic fireworks, the sparkle in her eyes from the flashes as each one was set off, and the excitement in her voice as she would squeal with delight. I did not want to ruin the fun for everyone else, so maybe it would be best if I stayed home.

I got up the day of the Fourth and went to have my quiet time with the Lord. "Help me, Lord, to know the best thing to do in this situation." The Study Bible I was currently using was missing. I had carried it to another room or somehow misplaced it. On the book shelf nearby was my old Bible, so I picked it up. As I opened the Bible to read, a small sheet of paper fell at my feet. It was a picture Mallory had drawn for me on the back of a church bulletin. The picture was of the American Flag. It stated, "To Mom." I had not used that Bible for a long time. Why on this day, the Fourth of July, did I decide to pick it up? Why did I not simply walk into the other room and find my Study Bible? Was it a coincidence?

I don't think so. What a special touch from the Lord to remind me that Mallory was still a part of our holidays. Her memories are warm and wonderful. I shouldn't run from them, but embrace them.

*J*oy is the result of knowing God is completely in charge of our lives. Therefore we can be content and joyful—because God rejoices over us!

As a young man marries a maiden, so will your sons marry you; as a bridegroom rejoices over his bride, so will your God rejoice over you.

IsaIah 62:5 (NIV)

The Unending Meatballs

BARBARA BRYDEN

uick! Go ask them to come to dinner," I whispered to my husband. "Hurry or they'll be gone."

"He never accepts an invitation from someone who works for him," answered Ken.

"Maybe he will this time. Go ask. We need to finish this conversation. If God wants them to come, He can change John's mind."

"All right, but he won't come."

However, John did accept our invitation. He and Carol and their two sons followed us home from church. "Please, God," we prayed on the way home, "help us find the words to tell them about You. And please stretch the food to feed everyone. A pound of hamburger, even made into meatballs, isn't enough to feed eleven. The seven of us could eat twice that many."

Carol and I chatted as I fixed the salad. Then with the table set and the food ready, we sat down to eat. I watched as the little dish of meatballs made its way around the table. There were fewer in the dish than when it started, but it seemed to stay half full no matter how many everyone took. I breathed a quiet "thank you" as I took some meatballs and set the bowl down. There was enough left to offer second helpings.

While the children played, Ken talked to John. All afternoon they discussed what was involved in being a Christian. Was it enough to just attend church? Did you really have to believe everything? Could you still act and talk any way you wanted to? It was almost supper time when they announced they were going to the men's Bible study.

It was quite late when Ken got home and shared what had happened. John asked God to forgive him.

We didn't know what else happened between God and John, but this man with a reputation for being mean and nasty became a loving, caring person overnight. Soon everyone was questioning him about the change and he shared freely about God's love.

A Visitor on My Doorstep

LARAINE E. CENTINEO

he urge to check on my year-old grandson, Joseph, nagged at me, although I'd put him down for a nap only moments before. *What's the matter with you? Guess I'm just an overprotective granny,* I thought, heading back to his room.

"Grandma's boy . . . why you're still wide awake," I called, standing in the doorway. "Come on now, go sleepy-bye." Holding onto the guard-rail, he bounced his legs and giggled as if he had plans of his own. Then he bent over and lifted something to his lips—a shimmer of silver shone between his chubby fingers.

"No, Joseph!" I called running toward him. But it was too late. The quarter he'd found in his crib had disappeared into his mouth.

I quickly picked him up and forced his mouth open. Searching under his tongue and along the inside of his cheeks, I realized, in horror, that the coin was lodged in his throat. "Oh God, no, help us!" I cried out.

Joseph started to gasp for air—long, whistling wheezes from his mouth. With trembling hands, I applied pressure underneath his rib cage, pushing in and upward. But it was no use. His eyes widened, and his round, little face began to turn blue. Then his body went limp. "Lord . . . do something!" I sobbed.

Suddenly the doorbell rang. . . someone to help! *Oh God, there's no time.* My stomach churned and my heart pounded as I raced to the door carrying Joseph. I knocked into an end table, sending a lamp crashing to the floor. Flinging open the door, a young man with a clipboard in one hand and a pen in the other stood on my doorstep.

"Help me, please, please," I pleaded. "The baby has a quarter stuck in his throat."

Without hesitation, the man dropped everything. "Hurry, just give him to me," he ordered.

I placed Joseph in his arms. Using a quick, firm motion, the young man pressed into the soft cavity under my grandson's ribs.

The quarter flipped out of Joseph's throat. It landed on the cement steps, rolled, and then rested on the pavement.

Joseph shuddered. He sucked in air—long, ragged breaths filling his lungs. Then the blush color returned to his cheeks and he began to cry.

"It's okay, Joe. Grandma's here, grandma's here," I said bursting into tears as I reached for him. "Thank you, thank you. You saved Joseph's life! How can I ever repay you?"

The young man looked at me and then at Joseph. His eyes softened. "That's okay. I was meant to be here," he said quietly.

"Won't you at least come into the house?" I asked.

In the kitchen, we sat and talked. He told me that he'd traveled for two hours from his home to collect signatures for an environmental organization. That day he'd been assigned to my area—arriving on my doorstep at exactly the right moment.

That afternoon, I said good-bye to the young man at my front door. "Thank you again for all you did." The thought of what almost happened swept through me and tears flooded my eyes. Holding Joseph, I watched the man from my doorway as he walked down the street and disappeared around the corner.

On September 1, 1998, our family celebrated Joseph's tenth birthday. What abundant joy that boy has brought into our lives. How we praise God for answering my prayer for help by sending a visitor to my doorstep—just in time.

Our Daily Bread

CHRISTY BREWSTER

 have two children who are close in age at eighteen months apart. When they were very young, my husband and I were in dire financial circumstances. One day, while he was out looking for work, I was busy looking in our cupboards for what I could fix for dinner. We were due to get a check the next day, so I just had to figure something out for the rest of that day. I discovered one can of soup; that would give us lunch. We also had some lunchmeat and a couple of slices of cheese. I thought, "Oh good, I can make a giant sub sandwich for dinner." I was relieved to have come up with *something* since, other than those few items, my cupboard and refrigerator were bare. My relief was short-lived when I remembered we had no bread.

While my toddlers ate their soup, I went into the small adjoining living room of our duplex feeling defeated. They looked over in curiosity as I sank to my knees.

"Lord, you taught us to pray, 'give us this day our daily bread.' I'm doing that now. Thank You for assuring me that You hear my prayers. Through Jesus, Amen."

Amazingly, the burden seemed to be lifted from my mind and I returned to the kitchen. I was curious to see how God would answer my prayer.

Before lunch was over, a knock came at the front door. I got up from the table wondering if it was yet another door-to-door salesman. Instead, it was my mother-in-law. She had a grocery sack in her arms.

"I can't visit, but I was just out grocery shopping and went to the bakery. Can you believe they had 'day-old' bread for ten cents a loaf? I couldn't resist and bought a bunch. I hope you can use some bread, because I picked up some for you guys. I just couldn't believe what a good sale it was!"

My heart wanted to burst with abundant joy.

His Overcoming Love

A. JEANNE MOTT

n a cold October evening in 1994, I sat at my desk in my makeshift bedroom trying to compose one last letter in an attempt to obtain some kind of justice concerning the worthless house I had bought two-and-a-half years earlier. My actual bedroom was the official "termite room" with a large, gaping hole allowing any curious wildlife to enter our home. Naturally I neither slept nor worked there. Unaware of the house's extensive wood-destroying insect damage, I had bought the house, not knowing a deceptive pest inspection report had allowed me to obtain an FHA loan. Two weeks after buying the house, I discovered the damage.

After two years of fruitless action, I chose to lose the house in foreclosure because three contractors and the manager of HUD told me it wasn't worth repairing. Not only did I face that, I also faced potential cancer. My surgery was scheduled in a week.

As I sat at my desk typing one last plea, I thought about how glad I would be to leave the stress and turmoil behind. I had been in such a frenzy to get "something done" about the house that I had little time for listening to the Lord. He had brought me through seventeen years of being a single parent. Then when I needed Him the most, I ran ahead of Him, trying to fix the problem my way. My life was at the bottom of the pit. As my mind and fingers raced with our dilemma, my daughter, Elyse, came in and sat on my bed to talk to me.

Over the next few minutes I listened to words all parents of teens hope they will never have to hear. "I'm pregnant," my seventeen-year-old child informed me.

I sat in silent bewilderment. My mind traveled backwards through Elyse's early years of vibrant life. And, of course, I wondered what I could have done differently.

Whatever brought us to this moment, though, was not important now. Nothing could undo what was done (except the more tragic sin of abortion). I knew I must accept and love my daughter unconditionally in spite of her mistakes. We discussed the available options—giving the baby up for adoption or keeping it.

There were hundreds of problems and details to consider. Elyse was still in high school and we already lived from paycheck to paycheck. The most pressing issue was that we would soon be evicted and had been unable to find a place to live. We both concluded we would want to keep the baby even though it would be difficult.

As I lay in bed that night, unable to quiet my racing mind and trembling body, I knew I must allow the Lord to lead me moment by moment. I prayed, *Lord, it will have to be Your grace and not my own efforts for us to be overcomers in this situation. I know this in my head but my inclination is to do things my way rather than wait on You. Please help me.*

A week later, after the surgery was completed, I rested at my mother's house, waiting and praying. Twenty-four hours later the doctor called with the bad news I had breast cancer. More surgery would be required and then treatment.

The weeks and months that followed were difficult. Recovery from the lymph node surgery was slow and painful. Because I was in a clinical testing situation, the chemotherapy I received was double the usual dosage with debilitating effects. Constantly nauseated, I had to take a medical leave of absence from work.

Our situation seemed so extraordinary it was almost comical. By God's grace, we sometimes laughed at our pitiful ordeal. But because of my illness, we were able to get a six-month extension to remain in the house. Now, completely unable to fix all our troubles myself, I was forced to surrender every aspect of our lives to God. Although our circumstances didn't change, God provided for us in a way that allowed me to personally experience His abundant love, grace, and mercy in a more magnificent way than I'd ever known before. God's provisions and blessings were poured out on us through our church family, co-workers at my schools, and my extended family (none of whom lived nearby).

People brought us meals, took me to chemo treatments, brought baskets of gifts, gave us money, and most importantly, prayed for us. Our minister and people at church found a new home for us to move into, and they, along with a dear cousin, packed all our belongings, moved us, and then unpacked. This wonderful family of God paid the rent, had a baby shower for Elyse, and continued to meet all our needs. Because of God's abundant provision, I never experienced the depression that one might expect in these circumstances. Rather, my heart was overflowing with joy and gratitude from experiencing God's love in such a personal way.

Three-and-a-half years have passed since my precious grandson was born. My daughter and the baby's father are happily married and living committed to the Lord. My son-in-law works part time as a youth minister and will go to school for the ministry when Elyse finishes college. She is studying to be an occupational therapist and is attending a private college with tuition completely paid for by scholarships and grants. With her busy schedule of school, study, and motherhood, she still finds time to teach children at church and works as a volunteer at a Crisis Pregnancy Center. I couldn't have a dearer family if I custom-designed it myself.

There's been no recurrence of my cancer and I'm once again teaching school, looking forward to whatever God has in store for my future.

Ever Wonder What You're Doing Right?

PHYLLIS WALLACE

ome of my "seasoning" as a young wife and mom happened in the kitchen! Feeding a family of six, three times a day, was usually fun and rewarding. But one day I'd had it in spades with everything going wrong. I pulled the old pity party trick, but instead of tea and crumpets, it was "poor me" played on trumpets! Standing at the kitchen sink peeling potatoes for the umpteenth time, I wondered just how such a mundane life had snuck up on me.

My marriage was spelled m-i-r-a-g-e. My four kids were acting their age. I was exhausted, grumpy, and feeling guilty about the whole mess. In fact, I wondered out loud, "God, am I doing anything right?"

It had to be serious, because I love to cook and I was resenting fixing supper. As I grabbed each potato and thought about the lemon meringue pie that was next, a piece of Sunday's sermon popped into my mind. It was a story about the great Apostle Paul who got really discouraged and how God sent an angel to cheer him up. I shot a prayer heavenward with a request for similar treatment.

Just then, the phone rang. I stretched the cord over to the sink and continued my culinary drudgery as I heard a pleasant, "Hi, Phyllis! This is Emily. I've been meaning to call you and thank you for some advice you gave us two years ago." She told me my counsel to the family regarding their depressed/suicidal high school daughter had been effective. "In fact, she's a music major in college now, writing songs. The whole story was a miracle. You were part of it, Phyllis!"

I thanked her, perking up a bit, enjoying the task at hand a little more.

"The other reason for my call is that a friend of ours down in Atlanta is writing an article on teen suicide. She remembers my telling her the four points you made and wants to use those in the column. What were they?"

Gulp! "The four points, Emily? First, thank you for calling. I needed some good news today. But I have to be honest. Whenever I encourage someone in a dilemma, I'm praying for clarity from God and matching up what I know about Him to the situation. So I don't really have any formula that I can just pull up for you. Do you remember the first point?" Before long we came up with what I might have said.

"Thank you so much, Phyllis. I'll give these to my friend. She wants to give you credit in the article!"

"Oh no. Please, don't do that. I think we can both see who gets the credit for this one, Emily!"

What timing! Had that call come two years before, it wouldn't have meant nearly what it did that day at the kitchen sink. My pity party was cancelled when all the complaining guests on my list left! They were replaced with a fresh vigor to pop those potatoes in the oven and start squeezing lemons. Maybe this is what they mean when they say, "If life gives you lemons, make lemonade!" I spell it lemon "aid."

Next time you're under with "poor me," skip the pity party and simply ask God what you're doing right. Keep an eye on the pie, but keep an ear on the phone.

He has a way of getting back to you!

The Whispered Answer

DEENA L. MURRAY

hat to do, what to do?

What do I get for my mom for Mother's Day? As usual I couldn't think of anything. So like many others, I headed to the shopping mall to see what would catch my eye. I'm not a very good browser, and I really don't like shopping, so I moved quickly from store to store and hoped that the "perfect" gift would jump out at me. Nothing seemed to be in the right colors, or style, and I came away from the mall with nothing.

A couple of days later, which also meant a couple of days closer to Mother's Day, I still didn't have anything. I said a quick prayer and headed out again. This time to some local shops. They had a lot of nice things, but nothing seemed right. Somewhere in the back of my head I kept hearing a voice of a whisper of an idea getting stronger and stronger.

In my church fellowship, we had been focusing on learning to hear God speak to us, and learning how to respond. I was beginning to think maybe I needed to listen to this whisper.

The next day, I felt silly as I headed back to the mall because I had just been there a few days ago and found nothing. I prayed out loud as I sat in my car in the parking lot. I told God how silly I felt and asked, "If this 'whisper' is from You, would You make it real obvious?"

I walked into the mall's music box store and they had changed the displays around since I had been there. And right out front was *the* music box! In the right colors, with the right song, and the right style for my mom. But I couldn't imagine why my mom would want a music box for Mother's Day. But the whisper said to buy it so I did.

I called her up that evening and told her God had picked out her Mother's Day gift! We laughed and she said she couldn't wait to see what it was.

On Sunday, when she opened her gift she was awestruck.

"Honey," she exclaimed, "how did you know I've wanted a music box ever since I was a little girl?"

Now, I was awestruck. Of course, I hadn't known. But God had!

My mother felt awed because God had known the unspoken desire of her heart. I was in awe because He used me to get it for her.

Peace

There's nothing like the relief of having peace. God's peace is something supernaturally given, especially in the midst of great difficulty or pain. He never worries, so neither should we.

You will keep in perfect peace him whose mind is steadfast, because he trusts in you.

Isaiah 26:3 (NIV)

King of Negotiation

PAM BIANCO

riving to work early one morning, my husband was car number four in a seven-car accident. He saw it all happen, but couldn't do anything to stop the destruction to our car—which, incidentally, is the car I usually drive. He had left his brand-new pickup truck at home because I wasn't planning on driving anywhere that morning.

When the insurance company took a look at it, they declared it unsafe and irreparable and wrote us a check to cover the value of our car. Unfortunately, the value of our car and the cost of replacing it with a comparable vehicle differed greatly. Having just replaced our 17-year-old pickup truck with a brand-new model, we were in no position to take on another loan. We learned one of the magic tricks of the insurance industry—it doesn't matter how well a car is maintained, whether we just bought new tires or whether the car is the most reliable we've ever had—it's all based on "book value."

So, check in hand, I went shopping alone because my husband was unable to take the time off to cruise the car lots. Knowing how easily I am intimidated by salesmen, I prayed hard. "God, don't leave me on my own!" and then I walked into the first dealership.

I explained what I was looking for and that I wasn't willing to negotiate. The salesman nodded understandingly and showed me to a car they "just got in." I believed it! It had a cracked windshield, made a terrible noise when I turned the wheel, and cost nearly twice as much as I had in my pocket.

I drove it anyway, actually finding it to be a very nice car. Nicer, in fact, than the one that had to be replaced. I took it to a mechanic friend, who determined that the noise was the power steering unit and after it was replaced, the car should run without any problems.

Upon my return to the dealer, the negotiations began. I'm sure they thought they had a novice on their hands, but they couldn't see that God was with me. My husband and I had purchased many cars during our marriage and never felt we had gotten the best of any deal. However, my calmness surprised me, and I knew I wasn't alone in that little cubicle dickering about that car.

I sat down and told the salesman, "I'll take the car if I can have it for the amount of the check in my pocket and the transaction can be completed by 3:00 P.M. when my kids get out of school." He chuckled until I told him the amount I was willing to pay—nearly half of what they were asking.

"Not only that," I added, "I want a new windshield and a new power steering unit to be installed before I take the car home."

By this time, the salesman was nearly hysterical with the preposterous demands I was making. However, true to form, he wrote it up for his manager and came back with a counteroffer.

Again, I stated my initial offer.

"I'm sorry, ma'am" he said, "but there's no way we can make that kind of deal."

Slowly, but with great calm, I rose from my chair, shook his hand, and let him know how sorry I was also that we couldn't agree. Then I turned and left his office, knowing full well I would drive home without that car.

Sure that my departure was just a negotiation ploy, he repeated, "We can't make that deal, but we'll be happy to discuss another offer."

I assured him it was no ploy. My calmness must have baffled him because he actually appeared speechless. Regaining his composure, he asked that I return to his cubicle and he'd talk to the manager again.

Three p.m. was fast approaching and I had to get going. But he came back quickly and let me know they had decided to sell it at my offer, after all. I wasn't surprised. I wrote them a check, left the car at the repair shop, and made it to my kids' school right at 3:00 P.M. A couple of days later, I picked up my new vehicle and went to the DMV to register it and make it really mine.

Even now, when I tell people about God's provision of abundant peace, I make sure they know about the day that God and I bought a car!

Positive Stress

EDWIN LOUIS COLE

fter restlessly preparing for a Christian Men's Event through the night, I called the office in the morning only to find some confusion and disorganization. No sooner was that resolved than a crisis call came from a member of a board on which I serve. I was already under pressure that day to complete a chapter of a book, but had a minister from overseas coming to see me, and was undecided on how to divide my time. Then a friend called for counsel. Each of my children called in succession. Paul had a business problem; Lois, a deputy district attorney, was concerned about an upcoming murder trial; Joann was having difficulties with her sons. The pressure was on.

At midmorning I still had not gone to the beach for my normal morning prayer. When I finally made my way downstairs, I found Nancy sifting through a stack of prayer requests that I was sure represented every ill ever visited on mankind. The newspaper on the counter caught my eye as I opened the cupboard to pour myself a bowl of cereal, which I discovered we didn't have. It was the day after statewide elections, and from the looks of the headlines, we would have some grim years ahead of us in government. I growled something about the world falling apart and felt the air around me tingle with static electricity.

Calmly and sweetly Nancy looked up from the table and said with a smile, "A wise man once said, 'Pressure always magnifies.'"

Pressure does magnify things. She was right. I knew what the sequence of thought would be next: that the world was terrible, I was doing it no good, there was no reason for me to be alive; everyone around me was in deep distress, and I was worthless as a friend, father, minister, and counselor.

Nancy's comment caught me, though. Instantly deflated from my tension, I sank down on a kitchen chair and willingly let her minister to me. The conference would be great. The ministry was going well. The kids had each been through the same thing before and were very capable of overcoming all. The board meeting was in God's hands. My friend could wait until next week. The book would get written, and why don't we just let ourselves relax and enjoy this visiting minister for a few hours. What a relief!

Stress is normal to life. Change is normal to life, and stress is normal to change.

Going Beyond Acceptance

NAOMI RHODE

hen I started my speaking career, my children were all in high school or college. They knew my fears and need for reassurance and growth in this area. Probably one of my most difficult speaking engagements was before the California Dental Association meeting in Anaheim in the early 1970s. I had a year and a half to worry, prepare my talk, fret over what to wear, and pray.

Ten minutes before the moment arrived, however, I began to perspire profusely and not a single word would come out of my parched mouth. Frantically I hid in the last cubicle of the women's restroom and in vain tried to control my shaking knees and get a grip on myself. Then the countdown began. Ten, nine, eight, seven, six, five minutes and I still wasn't any better. Things were getting worse. Four, three, two, one and I was unable to get out of the restroom cubicle.

Then I realized the meeting would go on without me. No one would even miss me. Someone would take my place. I could choose between passing on one of the greatest opportunities of my professional career up to this point and spending the next hour degrading myself in the women's restroom. Isn't it amazing to reflect on how our choices are made? That still, small voice inside that says, "Just do it one more time."

Two minutes later I walked up and stood behind the podium facing a huge auditorium full of people. Before I could say a word, my eyes fell on a handwritten note that said, "Dear Mom, We love you and are so proud of you. We'll be praying for you every minute." Unbeknownst to me, our three children had come to hear me speak and offer their support and encouragement when I needed it the most. The large audience was no longer my concern. I couldn't disappoint our three children who were counting on me to do my best.

Toss It into the Lake

ROBERT H. SCHULLER

his past week, I called on a dear friend of mine, Mrs. Putnam. She lives in Cleveland on the shores of Lake Erie. Not too long ago, at eighty-three, she fell and broke her hip. She said to me from her chair, "I was unconscious for three days; they thought I wouldn't live, but I did." Then she looked at me and said, "Dr. Schuller, how do you stay happy all the time?"

I said, "Well, for one thing I decided long ago to throw out all of the excess baggage of my mind. By that I mean the baggage of bad memories. Throw it out."

"How do you do that?"

Before I answered her, I looked at a picture of her deceased husband, hanging on the wall. He was a fantastic man, one of the great American lords of industry. I also noticed the picture of her son in uniform, killed in World War II. Now here she was, unable to walk. She repeated her question, "How do you unload the bad memories? How do you rid them from your life?"

I said, "Mrs. Putnam, can you stand?"

She said, "Oh, I think so."

I stretched out my hands. She took the blanket off her knees, and took hold of my hands. I held her tightly above the elbows and slowly led her until she was four feet from the window. And I asked, "What do you see?"

She said, "I see Lake Erie."

"I'll bet when you were younger you used to stand here on the lawn and throw a stone and you'd watch it fly into the lake."

She said, "Oh, yes, but I haven't done that for many years."

"Did you know that your mind can throw a bad thought a lot farther than your arm has ever thrown a stone? Mrs. Putnam, any time an unpleasant memory or any unpleasant feeling or a negative thought comes into your brain, I want you to stand, if not physically, at least mentally, right here and look through the window. With your mind, throw that thought through the glass until it sinks deep into the lake. Then I want you to sit down and read these lines." And I handed her a piece of paper on which I had just scrawled four lines from an anonymous author:

I shut the door on yesterday
and threw the key away.
Tomorrow has no fears for me
Since I have found today.

She said, "I can do it!"
So can you if you'll quit complaining!

Abundant Peace

KAY ARTHUR

will never forget the day I was saved. The night before, I'd been at a party. The only thing I remember about that night was that a man named Jim looked at me and said, "Why don't you quit telling God what you want and tell Him that Jesus Christ is all you need?" His words irritated me.

"Jesus Christ is not all I need." My reply was curt. "I need a husband. I need a . . ." and one by one I enumerated my needs, emphasizing each one by numbering them on my fingers. At five, I considered that I had surely proven my case, so I turned on my heels and went home.

For some time I had realized my lifestyle was unacceptable to God. I knew that if I were to stand before Him, I would hear Him justly say, "Depart from Me."

My sins were obvious. Even I could not excuse them. For the first time in my life, I had seen my poverty of spirit. Although I had tried, I could not quit sinning. Nothing good dwelt in my flesh, and I knew it (Romans 7:18–20).

I had made resolution after resolution to be good, to stop being immoral. Yet I gave in again and again. I finally concluded that there was no way I could ever be set free. I just wasn't strong enough spiritually to change. I knew I was sick—sick of soul. As a registered nurse I was an active participant in the healing of many bodies, but I didn't know of any doctor who could heal my soul. And heal myself? Well, it was impossible. I had tried.

After my divorce, I lived with gnawing guilt until finally my sin became an acceptable way of life. After all, how could my friends condemn me? We all lived the same way!

Some days I even thought, *If I could just be born again . . . have another start at life.* Then I would dream of what-could-have-been-if-only! I didn't know the term *born again* was in the Bible. Although my family was very religious, the Bible had not been a central part of my life. For the most part I didn't know what God's Word said. By this time I had lived for twenty-nine years, and no one had ever asked me when or even if I had been saved. I had never heard an invitation for salvation, nor had I realized that it isn't church membership or being good that makes us Christians.

Heaven and hell? Hell was what you made of your life here on earth. Heaven? Well, if my good deeds outweighed my bad, surely I would make it. At least that was what I was told! To be honest, I never felt that nice people were in any danger. No one around me had a burden for the lost. I had never heard a sermon on the need to witness.

When the morning of July 16, 1963, dawned, I couldn't face going to work. I called the doctor I worked for and told him I was sick, that I would see him Monday. I hung up the phone and got Tommy off to day camp. At loose ends, I decided I'd bake a cake and then take the boys camping.

Suddenly, in the middle of the kitchen, I looked at Mark, my younger son. He was so hungry for love! He clung to my apron. I choked out the words, "Momma's got to be alone for a few minutes." With that I rushed upstairs to my bedroom and threw myself on the floor beside my bed. "Oh God, I don't care what You do to me. I don't care if I never see another man as long as I live. I don't care if You paralyze me from the neck down. I don't care what You do to my two boys. Will You just give me peace?"

There beside my bed I found that there is a balm in Gilead that heals the sin-sick soul. There is a Great Physician. His name is Jehovah-rapha. But I would first come to know Him as the Lord Jesus Christ, the Prince of Peace. On that day in my bedroom He applied the cross to the bitter waters of my life, and I was healed of sin's mortal wounds. I had turned to Jehovah-rapha, returning to the Shepherd and Guardian of my soul.

Only one Physician can heal the ills of our souls. Why look elsewhere?

The Nightclub Dilemma

PAT CURTIS

y husband Max and I lived in a small Missouri town . . . the kind where everyone knew each other and each other's business. You knew your neighbor and people lent a helping hand. It was a great place to bring up a family.

We attended a small church in town where I also taught a junior high Sunday school class. Our children were active in church and took part in all the church activities.

Max and I owned a small background music company. We provided the soft music people heard when they went into a store or business. We had several clients in different cities and this required Max to do a lot of traveling, keeping him from home several days a week. After much thought and prayer, we decided to sell the business.

Max ran an ad in a newspaper of a large city about 50 miles away. The very first people who called about it bought it! They were a young couple who were trying to break into the singing industry.

They sang in any place they could get a job and thought this would be a good business to help tide them over until they could make it big. We spent some time with them, showing them how the business worked. Max went with the young man to show him the route and introduce him to clients. We enjoyed getting to know them and visiting with them.

About a month after we had sold the business to them, they called. They had gotten a singing engagement in a nightclub in a city about 30 miles away. They wanted us to be their guests and hear them sing. Not wanting to hurt their feelings, Max accepted.

I had very mixed emotions about it. I wanted to hear them sing but since we didn't drink, I felt uncomfortable about going. Max assured me, "We'll only stay long enough to order a soda and hear them sing."

I still felt uneasy about it. *I'm a Sunday school teacher. I teach*

13- and 14-year-olds who are at a very impressionable age. How will they feel about their teacher being in a nightclub if they find out? A battle raged in my mind.

When I shared my struggle with Max, he tried to put me at ease. "We won't be doing anything wrong. We'll just have a soda and listen to them sing."

But I wasn't so sure. "We may not do anything wrong but what if someone sees me coming out of the nightclub? How will that look to my class?"

The answer finally came to me. *I'll turn the problem over to God. Lord, I leave this up to You. If You feel that it won't do any harm, I'll go. But if You don't want me to go, please stop us from going.*

I immediately felt a peace flood my heart. I told Max about my prayer and then put the whole matter behind me.

Two nights before the singing date, our phone rang. Max answered. He sat and listened, spoke a few words, and then hung up.

"That was our singing duo. They called to tell us their singing engagement was cancelled! They said that had never happened to them before. They didn't know what to make of it."

Maybe they didn't, but I did. It was not in God's plan for us to go to a nightclub. I shared this with my Sunday school class. I told them, "If you're ever in doubt about what you should do, turn the problem over to God. He will never steer you wrong."

Someone Tell Me to Stop

LINDA CUTRELL

hid from my husband and family all my beer cans and the cardboard cartons they came in. I left the room to pop the tops so no one would notice I'd had five or six beers in an hour. I looked forward to 4 P.M., which was my starting time to indulge. This was the time I'd set in college to keep from getting too sick or too drunk to enjoy supper.

My drinking started at college and for many years I was able to handle it pretty well. Several years I went without drinking at all. Then on one of our family vacations to Florida, I had one beer. This one beer led to another and another and another.

Ironically, I borrowed a video about alcoholics thinking that my brother had a problem. After watching the video, I knew I was the one who needed help.

I reached out for help, but no one would say "STOP!" By now, I realized my drinking stemmed from a deep desire for inner peace. I could see that wonderful gift in other people and I envied them.

The first person I asked for help was a neighbor, Joyce, who was an alcoholic counselor. I had hidden my problem so well that she was a little skeptical when I confessed my dilemma to her. She advised me to talk to my minister, who became the second person I entrusted with my secret.

After listening intently, my pastor didn't think I had a major problem. He sent me to the third person, my family physician, who knew me well.

I didn't hear the word STOP from my doctor either, but he did recommend that I quit for thirty days to see how dependent I was. Before I left his office, I was trying to find a way around his advice. Why not try to limit my drinking to special occasions? What was I going to do with the booze already in the house?

A few days passed and I hadn't quit. My neighbor Joyce called me and asked what I'd been advised to do. I summarized their opinions and said, "I'm going to reduce my drinking to only special occasions."

There was a dead silence on the other end of the phone. She said, "You mean you've reached out for help and paid a doctor for his advice and you're not going to take it?"

She then informed me her husband was an alcoholic and he'd tried that approach. It hadn't worked. She continued by saying, "It might work once, Linda, but not for long."

Her words crushed me like a trash compactor. I decided that day to quit cold turkey. I had quit smoking in that manner; I assumed I could do the same with drinking. The next day at 4 p.m., I was on my knees seeking God's guidance for a plan and an inner strength to carry on. For a long time, it was a daily hurdle I had to face and conquer. I soon came to realize I needed God's help desperately and 4 P.M. became a kneeling time instead of a drinking time.

When I stepped out in faith, God enlightened me with the understanding I had two problems. One physiological, the other spiritual. I had lost that wonderful feeling of inner peace which God gave me when I had accepted Christ into my heart years earlier.

So, I began a relentless search for this priceless gift. My quest started by replacing the brown bottle filled with liquid with a black book with God's words in it. I joined an intense Bible study which required daily assignments. One of the first principles I learned from this study was that God keeps His promises. One of those promises is Psalm 37:4, "Delight yourself in the Lord and He will give you the desires of your heart." I did delight myself in the Lord and He began to give me my deepest desire—inner peace.

I also attended a healing service at my church. This service grew out of a Lenten Series about different kinds of healing. I had never heard of or considered a spiritual healing until this study. Our minister also spoke of a "Breath" prayer. This is a short, one-breath prayer you offer up every time you think of your request, need, or praise. At our last gathering, I knelt at the altar while eight people laid their hands on me. As a result, I finally relinquished my deep secret of needing inner peace.

My final step involved meeting with a spiritual counselor. Although she had been a casual acquaintance, she knew exactly what I needed. When I called her she said, "Linda, I know what you are doing. You're spending all your time doing good works thinking you can earn this peace you talk about. You need more quiet time—study time. You can't hear God's still, small voice if there is no quiet time in your daily schedule."

That was the key! I knew when I finished our phone conversation that my search was over. I was so happy that I was afraid to go to sleep that night for fear the wonderful feeling would dissipate. But it didn't. I asked for inner peace and got inner joy as a bonus!

God had been trying for ten years to speak to me, but I wasn't quiet enough to listen to His still, small voice. But now the time I spend with Him is the most treasured part of my week and life has become a very exciting journey.

The Lord's Battle

MARTHA B. YODER

hat do you mean I need further x-rays?" I was suddenly aware of what the doctor was saying.

"We see an unexplainable small mass in your right breast and need to get a more detailed study," my kind doctor explained. "We'll set up the appointment and call you."

On the way home I felt so troubled. "I feel like I'm facing a battle. It's probably cancer. Well, I'll not do anything to fight it. I'll just die! It's too hard to live with all our problems anyway. This will take me out of my misery." I was sinking into the familiar depression patterns of the past.

Once at home I glanced at the calendar. "Oh no, I have children's class tonight at church. I'll grit my teeth and do my duty. I can use the lesson from Second Chronicles 20 I used two years ago."

Usually I enjoyed my turn with my little friends but this night I felt so dull.

"Do you remember the song I taught you last time?" I asked. They all joined in singing, "My Lord knows the way through the wilderness, All I have to do is to follow." After singing it twice the words pricked me.

With a lack of enthusiasm I began, "Tonight I want to tell you about King Jehoshaphat. He was really worried. Three countries were planning to make war with him. What was he to do? He feared and set himself to seek the Lord. He called his people together to ask help from the Lord. As they prayed, none of them ate. He prayed, 'Neither know we what to do, but our eyes are on Thee.'"

I repeated his prayer for the children several times. Was that God talking to me through this?

I continued the lesson. "A man of God came to Jehoshaphat telling him, 'The battle is not yours, but God's.' The King was surprised, yet he began praising God with a loud voice because of God's message."

In my heart I sensed God's blessing coming to my very own heart.

With more vigor I continued. "In the morning the king called his army. 'I want all you singers out front,' he ordered. 'As we go toward the enemy I want you to sing praises to God. Everyone must hear us because we believe this is God's battle.' Jehoshaphat was rejoicing.

"When they arrived where they could see the enemy, they gasped. Every one of the enemy was lying dead. They didn't have to do a single thing to defeat them. Indeed, it was God's battle just as He had promised. What a great God He is!

"What a great God He is!" I exclaimed from the depth of my own heart again.

As I reviewed the story, I was pleased how much the children had grasped. But I knew the Lord had used this lesson to give *me* His blessings of peace and rest. The future of all things, especially my health, was in the Lord's hands. It was God's battle—not mine. I left the classroom with an abundant song of victory in my heart.

Abundant Provision

VALERIE L. BAKER CLAYTON

xcitement, anxiety, and great expectations filled our hearts as we prepared to move to Kailua-Kona, Hawaii, to begin our first staff position with Youth With A Mission. What a dream: two years in paradise!

Youth With A Mission does not have paid employees, but instead has volunteers who raise their own support through individuals who pledge a specified amount each month. This requires a lot of faith in both the Lord and in those making the pledges.

Though my faith was strong enough to believe God would supply our monetary needs, my own need to be in control was overriding my faith. I wanted the money to live on for an entire year *in my hand* before we moved. A lack of faith created within me a weakness to trust God with what I could not see. I just felt I needed to be in control and have the money first!

Many friends had blessed us with gifts of money, which soon became my personal "security blanket." Although it was a substantial amount, it was not enough to support us for a full year in Hawaii. After many hours with a calculator, I figured we would need approximately $300 a month more and we could move.

A few days after Thanksgiving, John and I shared with our pastor that we were relatively close to the amount of money we needed. Gordon leaned back in his chair and said, "I don't know how much you lack, but our finance committee met Wednesday, and we decided to support you for $300 each month. I hope this will help bring you closer to what you need." *Help?* This was exactly the amount we needed!

Within a few days of our arrival in Hawaii I sat working on our budget. Something was amiss. I figured twice, three times, then again. Each time it came out the same; I had miscalculated my previous figures. Somehow we were $2,400 short from the amount needed to live on for the next 12 months. My security blanket had a hole in it!

Crying, I stared out the window, "God please help me! I made a mistake. How can anyone misfigure by $2,400? I know that you promise to supply our needs. I say I trust you but my actions show I don't. Help me to learn to trust you more." I knew I could trust God. What I didn't trust was my own faith.

That afternoon, we attended our first staff meeting. The focus: finances. Vice-Chancellor Gene Early started out saying, "As you all know, the base is working on becoming debt free within the next five years. As leaders we have made the commitment to become personally debt free as well. We know many of you have financial problems and we would like to pray for you on behalf of your finances."

For over an hour, numerous people stood sharing their financial shortage while others prayed for them. Thinking of our own financial plight, I had the strangest urge to stand and tell my mournful story. But I didn't know these people. I certainly wasn't going to make my debut into campus life by standing in front of a room full of strangers and tell them my most personal money problems. What would they think? I made the decision to keep my money shortage to myself. After everyone had been prayed for, the meeting was about to adjourn, when Gene stopped and said he felt there was at least one other person who needed to have prayer for their finances. A long silence followed.

Again I felt the prompting to stand and confess my bank shortage. Again I reminded myself that I could trust God to provide the money. Once more Gene said he was waiting for one more person to come forward. Inside, I felt as if someone was pushing me from behind, but resolving not to stand up or to say anything, I burrowed down further in my chair.

I felt a strange sensation as if someone else was moving my arms and legs when I suddenly found myself standing with a whole room full of eyes staring at me, waiting to hear what I had to say. I haltingly introduced myself and confessed my financial miscalculations. Those sitting near us surrounded John and myself and started to pray. John could not believe that I had actually stood up and made such an announcement. Although he did not say anything to me, I could tell by the scowl on his brow that he was not too pleased with what I had just done.

Walking to the mailbox a few days later, I was rewarded with a whole stack of Christmas cards and letters. In the pile of cards was also an envelope from our home church. Tearing it open, out fell a note along with a check. Larry and Pat Barker, a family from our church, felt the Lord encourage them to share part of their savings with us. Out of obedience they sent a check for the amount the Lord directed. The amount? $2,400!

That first year has now passed and my "security blanket" account has long become empty. Our church family still sends us a check each month but that is not nearly enough to live on. God says He will supply all our needs and He is doing just that. Last year, I needed a security blanket in the form of cash in the bank and God supplied one for me. Now, our savings account is empty but my faith is full. No longer do I require money in advance to feel secure. I sometimes still worry about money and where it will come from. But when that happens, I know exactly what to do. I just exercise my faith in the Lord and in His perfect provision. God is the ultimate Security Blanket Account for me—an account which is abundantly full!

Perfect

MARY COTTON

o matter how hard I try, I can never please him!"
My fists balled up in frustration.

"How many times have you thought or said that?" the counselor asked.

"Probably every day of my life!" I began crying like a six-year-old. At that miserable moment I felt like a little girl again.

After three wet tissues, he asked me, "Would you like to change the situation?"

"Of course!" I was getting angry now. "Maybe I can disappear and eliminate trying to please him forever!" It was an extreme statement, but I was ready for extreme measures.

I had never measured up to my father's expectations. If I brought home a report card with an A- on it, he asked why it wasn't an A. When I worked hard to do a chore right, he still found something to criticize. He was a perfectionist and he wanted everyone else to be perfect, too.

I always felt so bad when I tried hard to please him and failed. I was tired of failing, but I didn't know how to change a 70-year-old man, so I was asking for wise counsel.

The counselor's next suggestion blew me away. *Will it work?* Desperate, I promised to try it that week when I went to Dad's.

"God, help me do this one thing perfectly!" I pleaded on my way to Dad's house a few days later.

"Hi, Dad!" I smiled and gave him my usual hug. He gave me his usual quick, half-hearted hug in return. We walked into his house for tea and chocolate chips, his favorite snack.

"I baked you an apple pie." I handed it to him, still warm, and thought, *Will he like it? I hope it's sweet enough.*

"Thanks. Your mother used to make the best apple pie I ever ate." For a minute he was lost in memory. I still missed Mom, too. And my cooking could never compete with the memory of hers.

The time had come to ask Dad the question my counselor had urged me to ask. My palms were sweaty and I could hardly breathe.

"Dad, what would I be like if I were just like you want me to be?"

He hesitated only a heartbeat. "Why, you would be just like you are now!" He actually looked into my eyes and smiled.

I walked around the table and hugged him, then said goodbye. I had to get out of there. I drove home in shock.

Does he really approve of me? Is he proud of me just as I am? Am I remembering the past incorrectly? Did I miss something by nursing my hurt feelings all these years? Or has he changed?

I don't know what happened but I felt a huge bundle of worries roll off my back. Sighing with relief, I thanked God for giving the counselor wisdom to advise me. At last I was free from the failure and insecurity that had ruled my life.

Two weeks later Dad had a fatal car accident. Even in the midst of my grief, I could rejoice that he and I had made a perfect peace.

The Peace of God's Assurance

JAN BRUNETTE

he light of the full moon shining on the fresh snow sparkled like jewels on a carpet of white. Each step I took led me into a new scene of beauty and example of God's design. As I looked into the streetlight, the gently falling snow floated and fell with grace, yet I couldn't hear a sound except the squeaking of my shoes.

In my mind, however, my inner screams and the words of the doctor overshadowed the quietness of the falling snow. "Tom only has two years to live" echoed over and over again.

"Dear God, what am I going to do?" I cried. "Where is all this leading us? How will I be able to take care of our four young children alone? Please give me the strength to see and accept Your plan for us—now!"

Tom's illness had already spanned a two-year period. He had been in seven hospitals, eleven different times. While we knew of his rare liver disorder, each doctor felt certain that many of his current problems remained unrelated to that. Time after time the doctors rediagnosed, tested, operated, and medicated. But they couldn't find any other cause.

Then a biopsy revealed that his liver had progressed to its final stage. Death was imminent. There was no cure for his disease. While the doctors hoped to ease his pain during the process, they knew his only hope was a liver transplant. Plans could be made in that direction but the waiting list for recipients would be too long. With only one hospital considered as a transplant station, there wasn't much hope.

For me, the thought of watching him suffer two more years was excruciating. "Dear God," I pleaded, "don't make him suffer much longer. If You are going to take him home, shorten his life as much as possible. He's already so thin and frail, I can't imagine him bearing up under the load."

The gentleness of the falling snow and the quietness of the night soothed my grieving spirit. Nearing the house, I felt certain of God's grace. As I watched the snowflakes float softly to their appointed location on God's carpet of white, a sense of His presence settled on my soul. I knew His love would float as gently into my life as those snowflakes. At His appointed time, all we needed would be provided.

In the course of the night, I awakened from a deep sleep to hear a quiet, gentle voice whisper within me, "Jan, there is nothing to worry about. You will have a house, a job, and money will not be a problem." Immediately, I returned to my quiet slumber.

In the morning, I recalled God's promise. I remained confident that God had spoken to my spirit and His overwhelming peace surrounded my heart. God would provide for us every step of the way.

Because Tom's illness would prevent him from carrying out his ministry adequately, we would need to change our lifestyle. The decisions and choices staring me in the face appeared beyond my ability to handle, but God had already promised His provision.

A move to Memphis seemed logical as many loving friends offered help and support there. Designated as the main breadwinner of the family, I needed a teaching job. Availability of such jobs remained more prevalent in Memphis than in the small town in which we currently lived.

The days passed and our move to Memphis neared. We would sell our house in Athens and purchase a new one in Memphis. Because of the inner peace I shared with Jesus, I knew every detail would be taken care of.

The church in Athens consented to purchase our current home. Nancy, a friend in Memphis, lined up a realtor there. Before I began looking, I told her, "I will know the house when I enter it. God has already selected and chosen the place we are to live, I only need to continue looking until I find it."

Within two days, the Lord revealed that house. Tom's life insurance paid for the down payment of our house and provided for the children's basic needs and their education.

God continued to provide for our needs. The principal of the school, who was a friend of Tom's, assured Tom just before his death that his family would be well taken care of. I was offered a job at that school on the day Tom died.

A friend told me, "Jan, I have never seen so many coincidences so close together happen to one person."

God's loving arms surrounded me continually. His provisions never failed. Even during the darkest nights, His presence dominated my life. As I look back, I can only say, "Although the years during Tom's illness and after his death proved the most difficult in my life, I wouldn't change a minute of it. The abundant spiritual blessings I experienced and the miracles I saw were worth the pain."

Rose Prayers

MARCIA VAN'T LAND

 was sitting by the kitchen table drinking coffee while our children were at school and my husband was at work. I looked at the two roses in the centerpiece vase. One rose was dried and starting to shrivel. Removing it from the vase, it immediately dropped some of its petals. I put four petals aside to represent my immediate family and then I retrieved my prayer list out of my Bible. Every time I picked off a petal, I prayed for someone or some situation. I scattered the petals all over the kitchen table as I went on my prayer journey around the world.

Now the very core of the rose was being exposed and the petals didn't peel off as easily. These petals represented prayers that were difficult for me to pray, like praying for someone who had wronged me. I prayed for pessimistic people who always seemed to live their lives in the basement. I prayed for all my sins even if I didn't know of them and I asked the Lord to show me what they were.

Alas, I was now to the inner part of the rose and there stood the yellow stamens—over one hundred of them—tightly packed together.

As I poked at the yellow stamina with my pen, I began to ask the Lord's forgiveness for my many apparent sins. I quickly reviewed things like envy, refusing to love unlovable people, gossiping, feeling sorry for myself, not making productive use of my time, being short-tempered with my family, not being a good friend, forgetting to reach out to lonely people, and wanting to do things for myself rather than letting God control my life. I went on and on until I came to the very core of the rose.

I left the rose petals scattered on the table all day. They gave me comfort as I went in and out of the kitchen. But I took that little core of the rose and put it in my favorite bud vase on my desk. When I looked at it, it became a constant reminder that God will always forgive my sins. He will always be near me and give me the courage and strength I need. The women who clean our house have wanted to throw my wilted rose core away, but it is still on my desk. That core represents how strong God is because it is very difficult to crush or break.

When our children came home from school, they all said, "Mom, what are you doing?"

When I told them, it made some sense to them. We went outside and each child picked a rose, took it in the house and began to take the petals off one by one. Soon the table was full of yellow, red, and white rose petals. We enjoyed the strong fragrance and looked up "fragrance" in the concordance of my Bible. The one text that applied to us was found in II Corinthians 2:14-15: "But thanks be to God who always leads us in triumphal procession in Christ and through us spreads everywhere the fragrance of the knowledge of Him. For we are to God the aroma of Christ among those who are perishing."

"Wow! We are like roses!" we all cried.

Then we took a beautiful red rose bud and put it in the center of the table. Over and over again we were reminded the bud represented how Christ died for all our sins.

A few days later our eight-year-old was outside by herself. I saw her pulling petals off a rose and seemingly talking to herself. In her own way she was pulling the petals off and praying for some of her old friends. She came into the house with tears streaming down her face. She was praying for a friend in Washington whose mom had been killed in a car wreck. I consoled her as best I could and explained that God wants us to pray for the hurts in other people's lives. By praying for them, we are helping them to get through the hurts in life.

After that, all our family saw the roses in our garden in a completely different way. And it all started with God abundantly using a wilted rose.

Patience

$\mathcal{W}$hy is it that patience is what we always pray for, yet resist when God brings opportunities to practice it? Patience is certainly something God gives, as we relax in His sovereign power.

A man's wisdom gives him patience;
it is to his glory to overlook an offense.

Proverbs 19:11 (NIV)

The Sonar Fish Finder

MAX LUCADO

'm not one to complain about new inventions that make life easier. I love our toasters, hair dryers, calculators. I think they make the little snags smoother in our day-to-day rituals. Yes, I like new ideas. . . . But this time we've gone a little bit far.

It's called the sonar fish finder, and it looks like a hair dryer. You put the nose end under the water and pull the trigger. A digital board responds to sensors on the nose, which in turn respond to the presence of fish. Gotcha! The poor little gilled creatures are victims of a radar system as advanced as anything used in World War II.

But the real loser isn't the fish. It's the fisherman. I haven't done a lot in my life, but one thing I have done is fish. My father is hooked on fishing. In fact, I can't remember a single vacation during which we didn't fish. Our fishing was as consistent as Hank Aaron's bat. Hours on end. Riverbanks. Trout jumping. "Shhh, you'll scare the fish." Wet tennis shoes. Corks bobbing. Up early. Fifteen horsepower motor. Minnows. Worms. Hooks. Stringers. Photographs. And man-to-man talks. (A fishing pole does wonders for conversation.) You name it, we talked about it. Football, girls, school . . . God. There's always time to talk when fishing.

You see, it never really matters if you catch any fish. Oh, sure, that's what everyone asks you: "What did you catch?" But the beauty of fishing is not in the catch—it's in the experience.

And a sonar fish finder? Well, it almost seems irreverent. It's like a do-it-yourself wedding or computerized dating. It's like electronic pitchers (dads are supposed to do *that*, too!) or those false logs you put in a fireplace.

Fishing is one of those sacred times that must not be violated and cannot be duplicated.

What is your sacred time? Afternoon walks with your friend? Early morning coffee with your wife? Long drives with your son? An afternoon at the beach with your daughter?

Maybe I'm making too big a deal about the fish finder. Then again, maybe not. The point is this: People are priceless. We should never allow a gadget to interfere with the precious simplicity of waiting for the fish to bite. If my father and I had bought a sonar fish finder, we'd have caught more fish, but countless precious conversations would have never existed.

My dad. The greatest fisherman in the world? Probably not. The greatest father? You'd better believe it.

Dirty Windows

JOSEPH M. STOWELL

y friend Bud Wood is the founder and developer of what has become one of the finest homes in America for mentally challenged children and adults. Shepherds Home, located in Union Grove, Wisconsin, ministers to many who are afflicted with Down's Syndrome. The staff at Shepherds makes a concentrated effort to present the gospel to these children. As a result many have understood and come to believe in Christ as Savior and in a heaven that will be their home.

Bud once told me that one of the major maintenance problems they have at Shepherds is dirty windows.

"What? How could that be a problem?" I asked.

"You can walk through our corridors any time of the day," Bud explained, "and you will see some of these precious children standing with their hands, noses, and faces pressed to the windows, looking up to see if Christ might not be coming back right then to take them home and make them whole."

Their simple minds and hearts have much to teach us. We should be asking ourselves, *When was the last time we glanced toward the sky to see if this might not be that long-awaited moment when we finally see Him face-to-face?*

Here Comes the Groom

eople always ask me, "Where did you meet such a great guy?" We met at a wedding. Not our own. I mean we had a short courtship, but not that short.

This particular wedding united two friends of mine (and of Bill's, I would find out later). The groom worked in radio and knew us both; the bride was a member of my church, which is where the wedding took place.

As a never-married, over-thirty woman, I didn't care for weddings. No, it was stronger than that. I *hated* weddings. I would sit in the pew, watching the church fill up like the loading of the ark—two by two—all the while moaning under my breath, "Where's *mine?*"

The woman getting married was named Liz, which meant the whole time she was taking her vows, I took them with her. You know, just in case I never got to actually say them myself *or* as a means of practice, if someday I did marry. When the ceremony concluded, I noticed a handsome, smiling man about two rows back, all by himself. No ring on his left hand. Hm-m-m. I knew vaguely that he worked at the radio station with Doug, the groom, but little else. Determined to learn more, I headed in his direction, thinking, *Well, I can at least say "hello."*

So, I did. And he did. Nice smile, warm handshake. Then he asked me, "What is that sculpture up in front of the church?" That sculpture was a very free-form artistic interpretation of a cross, not an unusual thing to have in front of a church. But then it suddenly struck me: *This guy may not go to church. He may not know what a cross is. Hey, he may not know who God is! Maybe I ought to introduce the two of them.* Off I went, describing the cross itself, repentance, baptism, Acts 2:38, regeneration, everything this guy needed to know.

I went on and on, as only I can, while he was smiling and nodding and smiling and nodding. *I've got a live one here!* I thought to myself. Then slowing down to catch my breath, I said, "So, tell me a little about yourself."

"Well . . ." he said slowly, "I'm an ordained minister."

I was speechless. (This is rare.) "A minister?" I finally said, as a smile slid up one side of his face. "No kidding!" I stammered. "Did I get everything right?"

"You did well," he assured me, and we both laughed.

One thing Bill found out about me right away was that I cared more about his relationship with God than any potential relationship with me. And that was exactly what attracted him to me. That, and my level of self-acceptance. And my laugh!

We stood there and talked in the sanctuary until it was empty, and I realized I didn't have the faintest idea where the wedding reception was. Bill had saved the directions and said, "Why don't you follow me?" Happy to.

At the reception, we kept an eye on each other as we mingled around the room, finally ending up at the same table. (Imagine that.) More talking, more sharing, then finally we exchanged business cards, and I said, "Call me sometime."

Now came the Big Wait. Four or five days later (not wanting to appear overanxious, he said), Bill called. I wasn't home, but my answering machine was. I can still remember coming in and finding the usual 0 replaced with a 1. For a single woman who had not dated in years, any night without a goose egg on the machine was a good night!

The message was short and sweet. A warm voice with a Kentucky twang said, "I wondered if you might like to go to dinner sometime next week?" I might. "Please give me a call back, Liz," were his final words. Not wanting to appear overanxious either, I waited four or five seconds before dialing his number.

Our first date came two weeks later, our wedding date was exactly eight months after that. (The only reason we waited that long is it takes a while to special order a custom-built size 20 wedding gown!) We'll be forever grateful to Liz and Doug for inviting both of us to their wedding, never dreaming that one ceremony would lead to another.

Prudence, Patience, and Praise

MARLENE BAGNULL

ouble coupons—up to and including $1!"
Obviously I wasn't the only couponer who had read the ad, for the supermarket was jammed with women holding fistfuls of coupons—many of them trailed by children whose little hands kept eagerly reaching for things on the shelves.

By the time I made it down aisle four I was beginning to wonder, "Is this even worth it? A lot of the things I need are already gone and, as always, I feel tense having to consider the importance of each item. Just because I have a coupon doesn't necessarily mean it's a bargain!" My frustration increased as I hurried down each aisle.

With only one aisle to go, I noticed the long lines at the checkout. "Go take the cart and stand in the shortest line with your brother," I instructed my nine-year-old daughter, Debbie, as I darted off to get the last few things on my list.

By the time I get done, Debbie will have us ready to be checked out, I thought to myself rather smugly. I noticed, however, that each time I returned to deposit an armload of groceries and look for several more items, the line had scarcely moved.

Thirty minutes later after finishing my shopping, I was still waiting in line.

Impatiently I shifted my weight from one foot to the other. For the third time I reminded Debbie and Robbie that if they didn't behave they wouldn't get any ice cream when we got home.

When we get home! I glanced at my watch—again. I couldn't help but observe that others were doing the same thing. The lines moved at an intolerably slow pace. I could feel the impatience and annoyance of the other customers growing, along with my own. Although the supermarket boasted of having the latest electronic check-out system, it obviously wasn't a time-saver. "This will certainly be the last time I shop here," I mumbled to myself, "even if they offer triple coupons!"

I was ready to add my complaints to the customers standing around me, when suddenly I remembered something I had prayed that morning. "Lord, help me be sensitive today to the needs of the people I meet. And help me be a positive witness to them."

I gulped. *Here's just the opportunity I prayed for.* "But, Lord," I argued, "You know I have just as much or more of a problem with impatience and waiting than anyone else. And You also know that I have to get home if we're going to get to church on time tonight."

I didn't have to wait for a reply. I knew God had me just where He wanted me—where He could put to the test the biblical principles I sought to teach others.

I laughed to myself. *The Lord certainly has a sense of humor, whether or not I always appreciate it,* I mused.

"This is ridiculous," the woman standing behind me almost growled. "I'm going to let them know just how I feel when I get up to that clerk."

There was no mistaking the anger in her eyes; but underneath it I could see the tears welling up from the pressure she was feeling, particularly as her two youngsters took advantage of the situation.

Sending up a prayer for help, I replied in a quiet and amazingly calm voice, "I know. I don't need to waste all this time waiting either, but I guess the Lord knew this was the only way He could get me to slow down today."

She was taken back by my words and didn't respond. Yet I felt the immediate impact that my mention of the Lord's name had on her and on those standing near us. The tension seemed to lift a little. Even the lines seemed to begin to move a bit faster as I prayed for both the customers and the clerks.

As my order was finally checked out along with my sixteen dollars in coupon savings, I headed home rejoicing about the more important savings I'd witnessed. A difficult situation had been redeemed. The impatience and annoyance I'd felt had been replaced by a song in my heart. And, though only the Lord knows, the first notes of that heavenly melody may have begun to abundantly play in someone else's heart as well.

When Strawberries
Taught Me Patience

DORIS C. CRANDALL

slipped into the kitchen and began lunch preparations. My husband and son would be home promptly at 12:10, and I needed to have the food on the table so they could get back to work on time.

I took a knife from the drawer, leaving it open so my disabled sister, Lottie, couldn't hear it squeak as it closed. If she heard me in the kitchen, she'd be right in to help me cook. With her help it took me twice as long to make a meal.

A stroke had left her with very little use of her left arm and leg, and we'd moved her in with us so I could care for her.

I'd finished peeling the first potato when I heard the thud-drag of Lottie's right foot as she dug her heel into the carpet and forced her wheelchair forward.

"What can I do to help?" she asked. She couldn't use a knife, and she might get burned on the cooktop or the oven.

"Oh, nothing," I replied, "I have it pretty well under control." I looked at her and smiled.

She loved to cook and her face showed disappointment. That look seared my soul and I could barely stop my tears. With effort, Lottie turned her wheelchair around and started back to her room.

"Wait," I called as I saw her slumped shoulders. I opened the refrigerator and noticed a quart basket of strawberries I'd bought to make a pie. *Maybe Lottie can stem the strawberries with a spoon,* I thought.

Lottie wheeled to the sink, washed the strawberries and blotted them with a paper towel. Placing them in her lap, she took them to the kitchen table. She returned for a spoon, inched her way back and began to dig out the stems.

"We'll work till Jesus comes," I heard her hum happily.

Suddenly, it occurred to me how selfish I'd been. I'd denied her the pleasure of working because I was in a hurry. *What would*

Jesus do? I questioned myself. *He'd have started earlier and been abundantly patient.*

From then on, I decided to plan my meals so there'd be something Lottie could prepare, too.

The Stamp of God

GLENDA GORDON

ast night, I had to mail an unexpected but important bill and didn't have a stamp. I thought, *Someone here at Bible Study should have just one stamp I can use.* As our group ended, I managed to catch several of our members and ask if they had a stamp. No one did. Although *something* told me to go to a different post office, I went to the nearest one, hoping to buy a single stamp. The lobby was locked. *All right, I'll go to the other one. That lobby is probably open. I should have gone there first, anyway.* At this point, I was only mildly annoyed.

When I got there, the lobby was open! I was relieved. However, the only single-stamp dispenser there was out of stamps and I only had $1.15. The next cheapest item in their vending machines was $1.90. At that point, I became thoroughly annoyed.

Of all the stamp dispensers to run out, why does it have to be this one? Why don't they keep this one stocked up? I fumed, fussed, ranted, and raved for several mad minutes.

A short time later, an older man came in to check his mail but he didn't have any stamps. A few minutes after him, a college student stopped by to mail some letters, but he didn't have any stamps, either. After the second person had left, I really ranted and raved. I snapped, "It's 10:00 at night! I'm going to get charged extra if I don't get this in the mail tonight! How am I going to get this mailed?"

I began to walk around the floor in circles, loudly grumbling to myself and God. I finally demanded, "Where am I going to find a stamp at this time of the night!?"

At that moment, I happened to glance under the counter across the room and saw something that looked suspiciously like a stamp. Or maybe it was only the extra piece of leftover paper that's shaped like a stamp. I looked around, walked over to the counter, and picked it up. It was a brand new, first-class stamp! I'm sure the man who came in a few moments later didn't understand why I was grinning like a Cheshire cat and dancing around the post office licking this stamp!

I dropped the stamped envelope in the mail slot with a triumphant flourish of my hand and a big grin. Then I stopped to ponder my silliness and lack of faith. Isn't impatience and doubt just like me? But isn't abundance just like God?

Desperation Turned into Inspiration

Jennifer Botkin Phillips

 drove hurriedly to my weekly talk radio show in Pomona, New York. My thoughts jumped to my scheduled show that afternoon and my exciting guest. Billy Porter was a Broadway star and the lead in "Jesus Christ Superstar" playing at the Helen Hayes Performing Arts Theater in Nyack. I had worked hard to get him and was looking forward to the interview.

Running late, I cut the corner onto the New York State Thruway too quickly. Bump. Bump. Within seconds, it was clear the subsequent thudding needed investigating. Pulling over and hopping out it was evident I was going no farther. The back right-hand tire was flat.

"Oh, no," I gasped. "Not now. Not here on the on ramp to the Thruway with trucks plowing up the grade and cars whisking past at record speeds. There goes my radio career." Unreliable talk show hosts don't go very far, and right now it was clear I wasn't going anywhere very fast.

A frantic glance at my watch showed 2:20 P.M. On a normal day, that would be plenty of time to drive the twenty minutes to the radio station and collect my thoughts before going live at the microphone at 3:00 P.M. But this was not a normal day. If the flat wasn't changed in the next few minutes, I'd miss my show and perhaps jeopardize my future.

"But, no, that's not going to happen," I battled inside. God had clearly enabled me to persevere in radio as a "social commentator" over the past year. He surely wouldn't take this from me just when things were getting going.

Grabbing my cell phone, I called Kathy, the station secretary. "I'll be there as soon as I can," I tried to calmly convey. Kathy asked if I could change a tire. "Well . . ., I don't know how. . . . but, I can learn!" But, that thought quickly vanished. Health limitations dictated there was no way I could change a tire. She then suggested I call the New York State Thruway emergency. Once I got the patrol man on the line, he seemed more interested in my location than my safety or even rescue and passed me off to the New Jersey Police Department, concluding that my scenario wasn't in his jurisdiction.

With no time for arguing, I reached New Jersey's emergency service. They wanted to know if I had Triple A? I didn't. While yelling my location over the roar of passing motorists, the cell phone died. Tears welling up, I tried to put on my bravest face and lift my head. Surely, by acting confident, help would come.

Getting back into the van, I noticed the notes for my show spread on the seat. My heart sank at the reality that I could be stuck for hours.

"My guest is to call at 3:15 P.M.! I won't be there." As panic began springing up in my chest, I told myself, "Okay, breathe. Pray. Ask God to send help. Trust that He will." It sounded simple enough. But, there wasn't a rush of cars getting on the Thruway that afternoon and those that passed appeared to have no interest in helping a stranded lady. Between whimpers, I got back out of the van, lifted my head and shoulders and stood tall and smart next to the flat tire so I wouldn't appear vulnerable. "Someone will stop . . . won't they?"

Within moments, a pick-up truck slowed and a medium-sized man in faded blue jeans hopped out and bounded up while flashing a smile. "Ya need help, lady?" he asked while checking out the situation. "Ah, Ye . . . YES!" I piped. "I have a flat tire."

"Let me see if I can change it for you," he quickly said.

Surprised by his "get-right-to-it" attitude, I continued, "That would be great! I'm a radio talk show host and have a show to do in fifteen minutes."

Just then, a second much larger pickup pulled over and another man hopped out. This one was taller, wore a tattered checker flannel shirt, blue jeans with holes in the knees, sleeves rolled up, stubbled beard, and looked like he just fell out the door of the late night bar! *Oh, my Lord. I'm in trouble now.*

"Hey, Greg, what's the damage?" he called to the first guy. *Oh, no! Are these guys partners in crime? Am I going to be thrown over the ravine any moment only to be found in the spring?* In spite of my racing heart, I somehow found my calmest and cheeriest voice, "Do . . . do you know each other?" I stuttered.

"Yeah, he's Greg. I'm George. We work together at Lederle down the road."

"Oh . . ., I see." Whew. Lederle was the huge pharmaceutical company. Surely, they must be reputable to work there.

They worked swiftly. George loaned me his cell phone to call the station back. I gave my report and said I'd be there as soon as I could.

Greg, George and I chatted. Of course, I chatted the most. They asked about my talk show. George said how he'd be grateful if a man stopped to help his "blond" wife. I mentioned that it's particularly scary getting stuck on the roadside since I had been victimized by a violent crime twenty years earlier. They mentioned that people have to be very careful about trusting people.

I replied, "I know I'm going to heaven if something should ever happen to me. I hope you know that too."

George gave me a surprised glance as I went on to comment on my faith.

After thanking them, the most I could come up with was a magnet for each of them from a radio promotion the previous weekend. Before we all said goodbye, I said, "I hope you'll listen to me on the air today. God supplied me with my very own personal Good Samaritan story to share, and it's you two!"

About thirty minutes later, I pulled into the station parking lot. They reversed the programming until I arrived and aired my whole show at 4 P.M. The interview went extremely well. The calls came in. They let me stay on for two hours! As it turned out, it was my best show to date because I'd seen God rescue me.

What started out as a huge mess ended up as a real plus! God's abundant grace and goodness is amazing and I continue to bask in His blessings. The blessings of that afternoon still amaze me and have rekindled my faith. Never again will I doubt that God's love is more than abundant in all situations. Even my future in radio!

Kindness

$\mathcal{K}$indness is that ability to be sensitive to the needs of others. God abundantly shows His kindness to us as He generously provides for us. He wants us to be kind toward others by seeing their need and responding as He leads.

Therefore, as God's chosen people, holy and dearly loved, clothe yourselves with compassion, kindness, humility, gentleness and patience.

COLOSSIANS 3:12 (NIV)

Divine Assignment

LORI WALL

 always had the desire to go out on the streets to witness to people after hearing stories from John, a friend of mine who worked with teenage runaways in Hollywood. That opportunity came when a weekend jaunt to San Francisco with my friend, Olga, turned into a mini-mission trip. As friends prayed for us, we realized we were being sent out as "ambassadors for Christ." All we knew was we were to do a prayer walk down Market and Castro Streets, where a great number of homosexuals congregated. I was excited, yet nervous since this was a new experience for me.

Olga and I arrived in San Francisco by plane late Friday night. Thinking we paid for a shuttle to take us to where we were staying, we found ourselves climbing into a limousine instead. We laughed at how well the Lord treated His ambassadors.

At seven the next morning, we headed for the METRO to take us to our destination—Market and Castro Streets.

We decided to go down Castro Street first. As Olga began to pray under her breath, I sang worship songs quietly. We proclaimed the name of Jesus wherever we stepped. Along the way we passed a bar that appeared to still be open. I didn't notice, but a man in his mid-thirties came out and followed us.

I ignored his faint cries of, "Miss! Miss!" until Olga grabbed my arm. Frightened, she pulled me to her side.

"There's a guy following us," she whispered in quick breaths. When we came upon a small department store, she quickly steered me in, hoping he would go away.

But he still followed, calling out more loudly.

Finally Olga turned around and asked him what he wanted.

"Were you praying?" he questioned.

Wondering how he could have heard us, Olga hesitantly responded, "Yes."

"It's been a long time since I've heard the name of Jesus," the man said. "I'm a back-slidden Christian and want to stop living like I am."

Amazed, we went outside the store to pray with him as he broke into tears.

When we returned to Los Angeles and shared what happened, we couldn't help but laugh at how we tried to run away from our "divine assignment."

The Answered Prayer

MARTINE G. BATES

n 1993, we were waiting anxiously for the call that would restore my 15-year-old son to health. The year before, he had a rare disease that hit quickly, unexpectedly, and nearly took his life. It did take his kidneys. We all had tests done immediately to see if any of his close family could donate a kidney to him. For one reason or another, none of us could.

So, here I was, praying earnestly that a kidney would be provided for him—and soon. I took a leave of absence from my job to devote myself to prayer for the kidney we knew was coming.

One day as I prayed, I thought about how grateful we would be to the donor. The next chilling thought was that, by the time there was a donor, he or she would be in the next life—we would never get the opportunity to express our appreciation.

I had heard a minister recently expounding on the need for us to ask for what he called "crazy things." He gave several examples to illustrate his point. My favorite was when Joshua prayed for time to stand still so he could finish a battle. God granted the request, and Joshua defeated his enemies.

On that day, I began to ask for my own "crazy things." I began to ask the Lord to arrange for the donor to be in Heaven to greet us when we get there, and for some way to know that he would be there. I always thought of the potential donor as "he," probably because Benjamin was a male.

Recipients of donated organs are not told who gave them; only general information is available about the donor. There was certainly no earthly way I would find out his spiritual condition. I knew that, and I knew that I was asking a lot, but I also knew that my God was big enough to answer my prayer.

When the call came from the organ center, we joyfully loaded our already prepared clothes into the family van and set off for the hospital. On the way, we prayed for several things: comfort for the family of the donor, a perfect match for the kidney, and a successful operation. I had not mentioned my "crazy" request to anyone.

The day after the operation, I got an opportunity to ask the doctor about the donor. My heart broke as I learned that my son had been given the kidney of an 18-month-old baby girl who had died during surgery. Rejoicing for our good fortune was tempered by sorrow for the family who had lost a precious infant.

It wasn't until several days later that I realized how many of my prayers had been answered. The operation had been success-ful—Benjamin was soon eating anything he wanted. The match was perfect—Benjamin's body accepted the kidney immediately and has had no rejection. And I know that the little baby girl, along with all other babies, is in heaven. We will get to see her and embrace her. Maybe my prayer wasn't so crazy after all.

Max—The "Fast" Car

t was the ugliest car I had ever seen. A faded "For Sale" sign was barely visible through the dusty windshield of the old Volkswagen Beetle, resting and rusting on the side of the road. Day after day I passed it, wondering how long it would take for someone to make it their own. Day after day, it remained, like a lost puppy waiting for its owner.

Curiosity finally won. I had been looking for cheap, dependable transportation, and thought, "What can it hurt to look?"

No paint. No stereo. Torn seat covers. The road visible through the floor mats. A rusted trailer hitch (what could they have towed with a Volkswagen?). But it had a brand-new engine and was selling for a fraction of the cost of the engine alone.

We named it Max. I suppose it wasn't the smartest move to bring him home on my wife's birthday. It wasn't for her, but a day earlier or later might have been more appropriate. But now she had full use of her car again, and I had Max.

For the next eight years, Max was my constant companion. He was dependable, economical, practical—and uglier than ever. The paint was worse, the seat covers were almost non-existent, the floor mats were threads, and there was still no stereo. But he kept running. He took me from city to city, visiting posh office buildings and luxury hotels where I conducted my business. He seemed proud every time he had to be valet parked by a uniformed attendant.

One year for my birthday, my kids surprised me with a stereo for Max. They worked hard for months to pay for it—washing my wife's car and other assigned jobs to pay it off. I was speechless—and more grateful than I could express. But I knew the windshield leaked, and there was no antenna or speakers, and the door panels were missing . . . so I figured I had to fix those first or the stereo would be ruined by the first rain.

But I procrastinated. Three years later, the stereo still hadn't been installed.

The kids never said anything, but I felt guilty. Eventually, Max began to show signs of age. Finally, the engine gave out, and it was time to replace him. I couldn't sell the car for much, since it was now ugly *and* barely ran. Unsure of what to do, I began to ask God for direction. How could I replace the car and still honor my kids' act of love? What would I do with a stereo that wouldn't fit another car?

Several weeks later, I remembered Jason. The 15-year-old son of some friends of ours, he had been looking for a Volkswagen bug to fix up for years. His parents had told us a year before that he wanted a bug like Max—one to fix up, then use as his first car when he was eligible to get his license. He had been saving his money for a long time.

It was on Thursday when God sent the answer to my dilemma: "Sell Jason the stereo for what your kids paid for it, then give him the car for free. It'll help him, and you can use the money to buy a stereo that fits your next car."

On Sunday, I mentioned to Jason's mom what we were thinking—our first conversation about it in almost a year. She said that Jason and his dad had been looking at cars that week, and were making a decision that afternoon on one. But she would ask.

When the phone rang, I knew Max would be leaving us. Jason's family arrived and swarmed Max like bees to a hive. It was obvious Max would have a loving home. But that wasn't the end of the story.

"Jason, tell them what you did on Thursday this week," his mom prompted.

"Well, I had been trying to figure out how to get the right car, but I wasn't sure. I prayed about it, but still wasn't sure. So on Thursday I decided to pray *and* fast about a car—and today I got my answer."

Thursday! On that day Jason had prayed and fasted, and God told me to give Max to him. I never thought of Max as a "fast" car—but God did.

Abundant Grace

KAREN DYE

couldn't believe my attitude! Here I was at a Christian conference and I was fuming inside. I had been standing in line at the bookstore for at least 20 minutes and the line was not moving at all. I focused in on the operations at the sales desk and noticed that there were at least five people working with customers but the line never moved. I couldn't imagine what could be taking so long. I was anxious to hear the current speaker at the conference and so I became very judgmental and angry of the operation and the people involved.

As I stood fuming, the Holy Spirit began to nudge me about my attitude. I began to argue with Him. "Lord, I've come one hundred miles to this conference and I'm missing it waiting in this stupid line."

He seemed to answer, "Ask me for My grace for this."

"But Lord, they have the problem, not me! If they would only get their act together then I wouldn't have to ask for grace."

But gently the Holy Spirit continued to speak to my heart and I began to pray for the grace that God desired to give me. Almost immediately the line began to move, however slowly.

By the time I got to the counter, I had prayed for grace for a good ten minutes and my heart softened. The woman that finally waited on me was extremely frustrated because of a problem they were having with their credit card machine. Being a business owner myself, I was able to identify the problem and help them work out a solution.

I was able to calmly pay my bill and leave the bookstore. I breathed, "Oh, Lord, thank you for that time of asking for Your grace. Without it I would have yelled at the frazzled volunteer for sure."

As I walked back to my seat in the auditorium, the Holy Spirit whispered, "When you ask me for grace, I desire to pour out more than you need for the given situation!"

So often God uses the difficult situations in our lives to nudge us to ask for that wonderful grace. In His generous way, He opens the floodgates of heaven and envelopes us with it. It's one of His greatest pleasures.

Door-to-Door Service

LIZ CURTIS HIGGS

he truth is, I didn't always trust in God. Despite my parents' best efforts to raise a wholesome, small-town girl, I veered off track in my mid-teens and started hanging out with a faster crowd.

First, it was sneaking a cigarette out of Mom's purse. Then, it was cutting school for an hour, then an afternoon, then a whole day. I smoked my first joint on our senior class trip. Most of the kids took the bus to New York City—I "flew." A decade-long love affair with pot began, ironically, on the steps of the Statue of Liberty.

By my twentieth birthday, I was spending four and five nights a week on a bar stool, Southern Comfort in my glass and longing in my eyes. I found companionship in many but comfort in none.

As a radio personality, I traveled "town to town, up and down the dial" through my twenties, including a stint at a hard rock station in Detroit, where shock-jock Howard Stern did mornings and I did the afternoon show. As a one-sentence summary of how low my values had plummeted, even Howard once shook his head and said, "Liz, you've got to clean up your act!"

By the fall of 1981, I found myself in Louisville, Kentucky, playing oldies at an AM station and playing dangerous games with marijuana, speed, cocaine, alcohol, and a promiscuous lifestyle. I'm one of those people who had to go all the way down to the bottom of the pit before I was forced to look up for help.

Leaning over my "pit of despair" and extending a hand of friendship was a husband-and-wife team who'd just arrived in town to do the morning show at my radio station. Little did I know that the Lord would use these dear people as my "delivery service."

Although they'd enjoyed much worldly success, what these two talked about most was Jesus Christ. Even more amazing, they seemed to like and accept me, "as is." (Can you imagine what they must have thought when we met? "Now, here's a project!")

But they didn't treat me like a project, a package that needed to be delivered from sin to salvation. They treated me like a friend who needed to know that being delivered was an option. Simply put, they loved me with a love so compelling that I was powerless to resist it.

I remember February 21, 1982, like it was yesterday. It was my seventh Sunday to visit my friends' church, and by then I was singing in the choir. When we closed the service singing "I Have Decided to Follow Jesus," I did just that. Walked right out of the choir loft and down to the baptistry, as the whole alto section gasped: "We thought she was one of us!" Finally, I was.

I was delivered, from one location to another, from the gates of hell to the gates of heaven—"absolutely, positively overnight!"

Making People Feel Special

CHARLIE SHEDD

ne of the wisest men I ever knew was a big Swede who never finished high school. Why? Because things were tough in the old country, so he came to Minnesota. Could he make a living in the United States?

When I knew him he had became one of America's top construction superintendents. He supervised the building of what were then our country's tallest skyscrapers. And he took great pride in his finished product. Every one of his buildings was a true giant, with the forever look.

But he was even more proud of another thing—*he was a master at making other people feel extra special.*

I watched him as he worked with his men. Laborer, water boy, trained engineer, president of the company, no difference. After a few words with him, they all seemed to stand straighter, walk taller—and look at the smiles!

Up and down the halls of our church I watched him, too. Here I saw him as a genius with boys, girls, men, women. And oh, how the ladies loved him. They gathered around him like hummingbirds. Why? Because he had a good word for each and every one.

One day the Big Swede and I were on a trip. This was the time to ask him more about his people secrets. So he gave me a lecture on people-dealing, and it was one great lecture.

"On the day I left home," he began, "my father said to me, 'Son, I'm sorry you did not get a good book-learning. But you know how poor we've been. Okay, so you've got to make up for that some way, and now I will tell you how.

"'There is an old proverb you must learn and live by. My father taught it to me. His father taught it to him, and it has been a long time with us in our family. This is how it goes:

> Even an ass likes to think he is worthy
> to be quartered with the king's horses!

"'You study that, son, and I promise it will be even better than the schools for you. You will see. Learning that—and living by it—will close even the biggest gaps in everything you do.'

"So all the way to America, I studied about that.

"What I decided it meant is that even the plainest person likes to hope he is somebody special. All right, I would train myself to imagine what other people see when they look in the mirror. And my father was right. It did close the gaps.

"This is not easy," he warned, "because you've got to break the habit of thinking of yourself first. But if you can turn your mind in this direction, you will discover there really is something special in every person. And the more you practice looking for the good in others, the more you will see it quick."

Then he concluded his discourse with this gem:

"The secret is to find the good things and to give them back. I mean out loud, sincere, and very strong. If you will do this and keep on till it comes easy, then another beautiful thing happens. One day you'll begin to really love people like the Bible says you should."

I'm glad he made that last point. Without a real love at the source, a divine love, our words will not ring true. There is a chattery flattery which is strictly phony. But that's not for us. For us, loving with integrity is an admonition straight from the Lord.

The Nest on the Porch

LOIS ERISEY POOLE

hat late spring of 1943, a cardinal insisted that she was going to raise her babies in the nest that she and her mate built in the trellis on our front porch. These colorful squatters became very agitated when we opened the door or stepped onto the porch. The female cardinal flew from the nest, startling the interloper, while the brilliant red male perched in an adjoining tree and scolded the intruder. Soon, my mother was as agitated and worried as the birds.

Finally, after we ignored her pleas to avoid the front porch, she erected a makeshift barrier at the bottom of the porch steps and alerted each member of the family that the porch was now out of bounds and not to be used. However, children being what they are, we avoided the obstacle and walked around it or climbed over it. Exasperated, she piled boards, upended picnic table benches and any other ugly debris she could scavenge, and arranged it in an unsightly heap at the end of the sidewalk that led to the porch. On this lopsided detour she attached a hand-written, cardboard sign: DO NOT USE THIS SIDEWALK OR THE PORCH. PLEASE COME TO BACK DOOR.

I was ten years old and my mother's eccentric behavior horrified me; I was ashamed of her. Everyone in our little town could see the pile of trash that decorated our front entrance. I wondered, "Why has God chosen me for this punishment? Why was I born to a mother with such bizarre ideas? Why do parents insist upon doing things that embarrass their children and make them a target of torment from their friends?"

One day Father Gorman drove in. Mother ordered me to run out and meet him at his car to warn him that he must use the back door. Red-faced and filled with humiliation, I walked up to his car door just as he stepped out.

"Hello, Father," I said. "Mom sent me out to tell you not to use the front sidewalk or door. Cardinals have a nest on the porch and she doesn't want them disturbed until the babies have hatched and left the nest."

He greeted me, then gave me a strange look.

"Mmm. A cardinal, huh?"

I mumbled "yes" and, head hanging, I led him through the garage over the oil-stained floor, past the stacks of muddy rakes, hoes, shovels, and piles of dusty gunny sacks and opened the back door so he could enter.

During the visit Father avoided any bird conversation but I knew he had to think that Mother was weird because that's what everyone else in town thought.

One day on the school playground I was being teased with the usual daily taunts. "Don't go to Lois' house. Her sidewalk is off limits."

"Your Mom is really loony because only loonies would worry about a dumb old cardinal's nest!"

"Yeah! Jimmie said he can't even deliver the paper. He has to ride his bike around to the back door. He says your mom is nuts!"

Filled with rejection, my self-esteem lower than the hopscotch pattern drawn in the dirt, I was angry at my mother. None of my friends wanted to have anything to do with me because my mother was peculiar. Just then I glanced up and saw Father Gorman looking at me with a little smile around his lips. And I knew that even he was silently taunting me.

That Sunday at Mass, Father Gorman began his sermon.

"Kindness is shown in many ways and we humans always think of angels as heavenly visitors who are sent to protect or guide us. But now and then the angels are not sent—they're already here.

"I want to tell you a story about a woman who has gone to great lengths to protect the smallest and most fragile of God's creatures."

His sermon continued and although he didn't mention cardinals or names, everyone in the congregation knew who he was speaking about. He told us how, in the smallest of ways, we can make a difference in lives, just like that 'woman.'"

"Not all angels wear white gossamer gowns and have huge feathery wings and a golden halo over their heads. Some angels are dressed in oil-stained overalls. Some angels wear printed house dresses covered by an apron. We don't have to search for angels. An angel may live right next door or down the street or in a house on a hill where a barricade has been erected to protect one of God's gifts to mankind. And what we don't understand, we ridicule. When we're inconvenienced, we tease. But who do you think God's light shines upon? The angel or the taunter? I would admonish all of you to not be so busy searching for heavenly angels that you fail to see all the earthly angels that surround you."

Father spoke for several more minutes about angels to a congregation of humbled parishioners. Even my friends gave me contrite, sideways glances.

The torment from my friends stopped that Sunday in 1943. And Father Gorman taught me that criticism oftentimes comes from the foolish human desire to judge another person's behavior according to our own definition of normal. I also learned that true friends don't ridicule. True friends understand that finding the joys of life are personal and must be discovered in our own intimate way. He taught me that no one should ever be embarrassed by a kindness.

I had always known that my mother saw the world and all its magnificent glories differently than other people. But it wasn't until that Sunday morning that I learned that that difference was something to be proud of. Instead of feeling punished I began to feel blessed. After all, I had an angel in my house. An angel who cared enough to protect three little cardinals who, one by one, flew away to begin life in the shadowy, cool thicket behind our house.

His Voice in My Heart

JOEL R. WALDRON SR.

 n the early days of my ministry, I had no automobile when answering calls to speak. If I had the funds, I rode the bus. In the absence of this I hitchhiked to my appointments.

I once felt I should go to High Point, North Carolina, for a Sunday night service. I had an open invitation to this church. Arising early I began to hitchhike.

As the day wore on, I was not having any success at getting a ride. Just outside of Mount Airy, North Carolina, I looked at my watch and thought, if I catch a ride from here to the church I will barely make it in time for the service. I stood there about five more minutes without any luck. With a crushed heart, I decided that I had missed the will of God. I began to walk back toward town. I would get me a room and pray this thing out. I wanted to know why I had failed.

I had walked about twenty feet when the voice of God spoke to my heart, "I told you to go to High Point!"

With tears in my eyes I turned back and replied, "God, I don't know when I will get there. I don't know how I will get there. I don't know what I will do when I get there, but I'm on my way."

The very next car stopped. Getting in the car I noticed the driver was drinking. Normally I would not accept a ride under these conditions. But I felt God was at work.

In answer to his questions, I told him where I was going and my reasons for going.

All the time he was talking, he addressed me as "friend." He said, "Friend, when you get to where I'm going, you will be about twenty miles from where you want to be."

When we got to Winston-Salem, he said, "Friend, if you go to High Point, I go to High Point."

When we got to High Point, he said "Friend, where is this church you have been telling me about?"

Following my directions he drove me straight to the church

door. I thanked him for his kindness. He asked, "Will you remember me in your prayers?"

As he drove off into the night I immediately thanked God for him and prayed God's blessings upon him.

I hadn't known about it but the church had delayed the starting time by fifteen minutes. I was only five minutes late for the service.

Preaching was not difficult that night.

Rescued

JUNE L. VARNUM

nother sleepless night. *You might as well get up and do something. You sure aren't going to sleep now—it's almost morning. Have a cup of coffee during devotions, then work in the garden. Pull weeds, dig up and separate the bulbs and iris roots. Keep busy!*

I lectured myself daily, but it didn't seem to help much. Since my husband's death a year earlier, I couldn't get motivated. In truth, I spent a lot of time running away: coffee at Wendy's or a drive to the mall. I didn't need a reason for afternoon ice cream or coffee at another fast-food place—sometimes with a friend. I looked for almost anything to get away from the house and the constant reminders that he wasn't there anymore.

Suddenly the loud jangling of my phone shattered the quiet. *It's only 6:00 A.M.!*

"Hi, Gram. Did I wake you up?"

"No, Crystal, I'm up and having a cup of coffee. Are you all right? Is anything wrong?"

"No, Gram. I just wondered if you'd be able to cook a turkey for us tomorrow. I'm on the Student Council at our high school and we're going to serve early Thanksgiving dinner to the people at the Veterans Home. If you can, could you pick up the turkey at the school office this morning?"

"Sure, Crystal. I can do that. I'll run over before about 9:00."

My "yes" led to other early morning phone calls: "Gram, would you have time to make some cookies for the bake sale after the assembly this afternoon and bring them to the gym about 2:00? Mom worked late last night and I had a lot of homework and didn't have time this morning."

How did she have time for anything? She had a twenty-hour-per-week job, was in all honor classes, active in three sports, and several student activities. Her Mom didn't get off work until 11:00 P.M.

Another 5:00 A.M. call and I heard Crystal's soft voice, "Hi,

Gram. I'm sorry to call so early. Could you pick me up after school and help me buy materials for the Winter Fest candidate sashes? We need white shiny cloth. And, umm, would you be able to cut and sew them?"

I poured my morning cup of coffee, grabbed my Bible and journal. Flopping down on my favorite rocking chair, I began to laugh—right out loud. *Well, Lord, no time for mall shopping and coffee and ice cream at Wendy's today. Crystal is so fun to be with. Thank You for the times other girls on those committees go with us and include me in their chatter.*

The following week my garage floor was covered with poster paper, glitter, ribbons, spray paint, yardsticks, scissors, and jean-clad teenage girls. Their music echoed off the walls; their comments, giggles, bounced about like bright balloons. Occasionally, the kitchen door opened and one of the girls would call, "Gram, come see this. Do you like the color? Should we use more gold?"

How fun to be included in their Christmas tree decorating project. Their group had entered a decorating contest put on by the downtown merchants. The night of the judging, the girls invited me to join them. Bundled up against freezing winds, we wandered along the four blocks of sparkling, glittering, decorated trees. Sometimes a mittened hand reached for mine, "Are you warm enough, Gram? Are you tired?"

When the time came to leave, my granddaughter threw me a mischievous smile, "We're going to drag main street now."

The girls laughed as we piled into the car. *Lord, please don't let this be a mistake.* Crystal drove slowly through town as we again admired the decorated trees. Then she turned to make the return trip. "Gram, did you and grandpa ever drag the streets?"

"No, honey, this is my first experience."

A burst of delighted laughter rolled from the back seat as we sedately dragged main street. Two hours later, snuggled in my warmest robe, ensconced in my rocking chair, I sipped a mug of hot chocolate. All at once tears welled up and spilled over. I thought about the night's experiences—and knew peace and contentment. Swallowing the last dregs of hot chocolate, I whispered, *Thank You, Lord, for Your abundance of comfort.*

Gertie's Glasses

IRENE HINKLE FAUBION

t was a good catch—the most fish Jim and Gertie had ever caught in their big seine-net. It would make a big difference for them as they faced the problems of the Great Depression. Many men had no employment. Some worked on road projects for a pittance but most were on welfare. Jim felt fortunate to live so close to the river where he could at least count on having fish to eat and enough cash from selling them to buy a few groceries.

They were carefully easing the net up alongside the boat when Gertie felt her glasses start to slide down her nose. Not daring to take either hand off the net, she lifted her arm just a little to shove them back. Too late! She gasped as they hurtled into the muddy water.

"Jim. Oh, Jim!" she cried, "My glasses, they're gone!"

Jim gave a final heave, landing the fish in the boat.

He reached over and took her in his arms.

"What am I going to do?" she cried. "I can't read; I can't sew. Oh, God, why?" She remembered how long it had taken to save her egg money and buy those glasses.

Jim kissed her again and again. "I don't know, honey. All I can say is we know our Heavenly Father cares and has promised to supply all our needs."

The next day Gertie still felt sad. She was unable to return to her usual happy self. The loss was almost more than she could bear. It would take months to save for another pair.

Jim and Gertie attended the rural church where my husband, Wayne, pastored. On Friday as I was praying, I sensed we should go see them. When I shared my concern, Wayne agreed.

Gertie heard our car when we pulled up in front of their house and came running out to greet us. Giving me a hug she said, "I've been hoping and praying all day you folks might come by."

As soon as we were seated, Gertie told us the sad news about her glasses. "Pastor, what am I going to do? I can't even read my Bible!"

"I don't know, Gertie, but your Heavenly Father does. You have put your trust in Him. He won't fail you now. Would you like me to read to you from His Word?"

"Please do, it would be such a comfort."

He chose the eighth chapter of Romans; verse twenty-six was especially comforting to all of us as we sat there. "We don't always know how or what to pray for, but the Holy Spirit, who dwells within us, knows the mind of God and He will intercede for us according to His will." Wayne then asked me to lead them in prayer.

"Dear God," I began, "please help Gertie find her glasses." I couldn't believe I'd actually asked that Gertie find her prized possession in the muddy river!

The next day Jim and Gertie returned to the river. In the first catch Gertie caught a glimpse of something shiny clinging to the bottom of the net. Emptying the fish into the boat, they flipped the net over and felt through the mud and wet leaves. Jim finally located a firm object. As he carefully removed the debris, Gertie shouted, "It's my glasses!"

The glasses were not scratched; neither were they bent. With arms uplifted Jim and Gertie praised God who alone had abundantly provided for this great need.

Resting with God

Mayo Mathers

he headlights of my car were overpowered by the heavy black night as I drove along the mountain road. I peered through the rain-splattered windshield, unsure if it was my tears or the rain making vision so difficult.

Turning on the heater to take the chill off my heart, I wept. "Oh God why did this happen? Where are You in all this?"

I was returning from a visit with my parents and sister who lived several hours away. My sister had been severely brain injured in a drunk driving accident. For months now, I had grabbed at every tiny progress, full of irrational hope for her recovery. On this visit, however, I was forced to face reality. My sister would never recover. For the rest of her life she would require constant care.

Grief consumed me as I twisted my way through the mountain pass. Shifting to a lower gear, I heard a loud "thunk." Startled, I tried to shift into a different gear. Nothing happened. The car slowed to a standstill along the edge of the road. Thick darkness engulfed me as I turned off the engine and headlights. Now what?

Swallowing back fear, I locked the car and walked toward a faint gleam of light tucked back in the towering pine trees. It turned out to be the window of a small cottage. I approached the porch cautiously, hesitant to knock on an unfamiliar door late at night.

In response to my timid rap, the door swung open to reveal a smiling, middle-aged man. "Welcome! Come in!" He beamed. Though the cottage appeared safe and warm, I hovered near the door, still struggling with fear.

Explaining about my car, I asked to use his phone. When I dug out my calling card he objected. "Your call is on me. I get lots of stranded people knocking on my door out here. It's my way of helping."

My phone call to my husband went unanswered so I asked the

man if he knew of a motel nearby. "No motels," he said, "but I think I have an idea."

Before I knew it, I was being handed over to the elderly owner of a nearby fishing lodge who had a room available. She, too, refused to take money from a stranded traveler.

The "room" was actually a cozy cabin with one entire wall of glass overlooking a magnificent rushing river. A plump couch and chair faced a fireplace where a fire was laid, just waiting for a match. Such a cabin I could never afford, yet here I sat, snug and warm, surrounded by luxurious beauty.

Relaxed by the sound of tumbling water, I picked up a Bible laying nearby and opened it to Psalms 139. As I read, the third verse brought a grin of delight: "You chart the path ahead of me, and tell me where to stop and rest. Every moment, you know where I am" (TLB).

Looking around me I realized that nothing, not my sister's accident, or my car's breakdown or anything was happenstance. I may have felt as if I'd wandered away from God's attention but this lavish respite He'd arranged proved otherwise.

Before I fell asleep, I called home to leave a message on the answering machine for my husband. "The car broke down on the mountain tonight. Please come get me—but don't hurry. God and I are resting."

Goodness

Goodness is that ability to do the right thing at the right time in the right way. God is always good and He empowers us to make right choices—when we seek His "one and only" way.

How great is your goodness, which you have stored up for those who fear you, which you bestow in the sight of men on those who take refuge in you.

PSALM 31:19 (NIV)

Holey, Holey, Holey

SUE CAMERON

ot too many pounds ago I had three preschoolers. Back then our budget was tight and my jeans were loose. One morning I borrowed a car, loaded up my brood, and headed for Gemco. It was the store with everything: housewares, fabric, clothes and, way in the back, the lowest-priced groceries in town.

We went in for food, but took a tempting detour through the shoe department. The cart stopped itself in front of the ladies' socks. I really needed socks. I really needed groceries. I looked down at my neglected feet, then up at my three hungry children. No contest. My feet were definitely outnumbered. The choice seemed totally obvious and completely unfair. I knew other people with preschoolers who could afford socks *and* food. I even considered some of those people to be my friends—usually.

I glanced sideways at the other shoppers. Some had new towels in their carts. Others had name-brand shampoo that made your hair smell like an herbal garden. *I bet they can afford socks*, I thought. *They probably buy the fancy kind with cute little patterns. All I want is plain, white cotton.*

I reached for the package and examined it. They sure were white. They sure were soft. They sure didn't have holes in the heels—like mine.

"Mommy," my two-year-old asked, "you hugging socks?"

The baby squirmed in her front snuggle/carrier.

"Mom," Mr. Four-year-old informed me, "You're smashing the baby. Didn't we come to buy food?"

I looked into the eyes of my trusting children and sighed deeply. Reluctantly I hung the package back on the hook. Then I squared my shoulders and pointed the cart toward the grocery section. But before I gave it a forward push, I said a quick prayer. I did not kneel. I did not wail. I did not close my eyes. I just lifted a thought to the One who always hears. "God, I need socks."

The next day I answered an unexpected knock on the front door. I opened it to see Shirley, a lady from church.

"Hi, Sue," she said. "My daughter-in-law works at a sporting goods store and has access to some clothes. I thought you might be able to use them."

"Great!" I said. "I love hand-me-downs."

"Most of these are new," she explained. "Overstocks, discontinued items, or returns."

Shirley brought in four large, black, plastic trash bags.

"Thanks for thinking of me," I said, waving, as she backed out of the driveway.

The kids gathered around as I loosened the knot on the first bag.

"Isn't it nice when people give us clothes?" I said.

Mr. Four-year-old peered into the bag. "These aren't clothes," he announced. "It's nothing but a great big bag full of socks."

I gathered them into my arms—the children, not the socks—and hugged them. Isn't God abundantly good?

He Directs Our Steps

DEBBIE ALLEN

y husband Tim and I were at the beach in Grafton Lakes State Park, New York, when we decided to go swimming. Even though Tim quickly swam into the water, I hesitated. "It's too cold!" I called to Tim. But he wanted me to join him out by the ropes.

As I waded slowly into the water, I stubbed my toe on something on the bottom of the lake. Usually I would have investigated, but I had examined similar lumps in the past, and they had always turned out to be sandbags holding down ropes. So, cold and dazed, I continued wading into the deep water.

A minute or so passed. A little girl swam toward us, then screamed. She had stepped on something, too.

"Tim, you better go down and see what that is," I said. "What if it's a kid or something?"

Tim dove under the water and came up holding the body of a child. "Lifeguard!" he yelled and ran toward shore.

I was horrified, for a split second paralyzed, as I realized I had stepped on a body on the bottom of the lake . . . the body of a child. Now that child might be dead because I hadn't investigated sooner. Dead because of me!

Within moments, the child's mother screamed from nearby. She could see Tim handing over her five-year-old son to the lifeguard. While an emergency medical technician cleared the boy's throat and gave him oxygen, I held the hysterical young mother in my arms and prayed. I whispered encouragement into her ear and asked for her son's name. She choked out, "Eric."

Eric lay on the sand, his body blue, his arms stiff. His eyes had rolled back in his head and his teeth protruded from his drawn and bony face.

With a boldness from God, I reached down and laid my hand on Eric. I prayed: "I speak life into this child" and spoke Jesus' name over and over again. I prayed for what seemed a long time. Thankfully, no one told me to stop.

Hoarse groans, then screams, suddenly erupted from Eric as he tried to take in the oxygen despite the huge amount of water in his lungs. Finally he started to breathe in the oxygen, and by the time the ambulance came, he was breathing on his own.

At the hospital that night, his vital signs were still very poor. The doctors feared he had brain damage. The Lord directed Tim and me to continue praying and we called others to pray.

The next day I went to the hospital. I was surprised when I walked into Eric's room. He was not the grotesque figure I had seen the day before, but a beautiful boy, with wavy brown hair and huge brown eyes. He was laughing and eating a hot dog. Completely healed! Completely normal!

Now, when I start to fear, I remember that day: how God directed my underwater steps, how His timing was perfect—never early, never too late.

My Secret Sanctuary

CHARLOTTE ADELSPERGER

n 1966, I drove home from another discouraging doctor's appointment. A flood of painful emotion tightened my chest. "Why can't I have a baby?" I cried out to God. "All those tests—the pain and waiting have gone on too long!" Disappointed that God didn't answer me, I longed for a private place to just let loose and cry. I passed St. Andrew's Episcopal Church in Kansas City where I had visited years before. I felt drawn to go in but practical thinking held me back. *I can pray at my own church or in my own living room. Why go here?* But before I realized it, I had turned in to the church parking lot.

My legs felt heavy as I walked cautiously into the building. I slipped into a pew, and absorbed the beauty of the sanctuary. To my relief, I was alone—just the Lord and me. Then I knelt and focused on the cross of Christ, my Lord and Savior. He would be my listener, my intercessor. Silently, I told the Lord how much I wanted to be a mother, spilling out my fears and worries. Then I released them all into His care. A gentle peace flowed through me. I left the church with a lighter step. Somehow I knew God had heard and cared.

But the uncertain journey continued. I underwent more medical tests. Still no pregnancy. My husband Bob's face revealed sadness. Yet he remained cheerful and gave me constant loving support.

A year later in July, my doctor scheduled me for surgical studies in the hospital. Just a few days before I was to go in, I was reading on our back porch when a deep sense of God's presence swept over me. Like a personalized message, memorized Scripture came to me: "Trust in the Lord with all your heart and lean not on your own understanding . . ." (Proverbs 3:5a NIV). I was filled with an incredible assurance that I would become a mother! I didn't know how I knew, but I knew it was true! *Yes, I'm going to be a mother!*

I called to Bob who was mowing the lawn. "Hey, I've got to tell you something!" He stopped and hurried up on the porch.

"It may sound crazy, but I've just experienced the most wonderful peace from God. I believe with all my heart that God is hearing our prayers. It's like He's telling me we will be parents!" Bob hugged me but I knew he had his doubts. Later that evening I wrote down the date, July 22, 1967, along with notes about the experience and the Scripture. Prayerfully, I placed the paper in my Bible. It dawned on me that I had just discovered another "sanctuary"—our screened-in back porch.

A few days later our pastor visited me in my hospital room before surgery. I told him all about my experience. He responded with a prayer for Bob and me as "the couple who dares to dream." In that moment, I experienced an additional "sanctuary."

Unfortunately, the post-surgical reports gave us little hope for conceiving. That hurt. Hadn't God assured me of His promise? Yet Bob and I continued to pray, trusting God. Then a strange thing happened. In September I noticed indications that I might be pregnant. *Is this one of those "false" pregnancies?* I wondered.

A few weeks later I went back to the doctor. After an examination and pregnancy test, he said, "Charlotte, I can't believe it but you're pregnant!" He expressed hesitation about the months ahead, but I was awestruck, and began to cry. "God is so good!" I blurted out.

Of course, Bob and I were elated to see how God was working in our lives. We thanked Him over and over. Every day I woke up with the wonderful realization: *I'm going to be a mother!* Many people, including Bob, prayed for the health of our baby and for me. My doctor checked me often but it was a smooth pregnancy!

I shall never forget the morning of May 9, 1968, when I gave birth to a healthy baby girl, Karen Sue Adelsperger. I watched her delivery by mirror and burst into tears of joy. Even the doctor was excited. He told the nurses, "I'm going to carry the baby to the nursery myself." When the doctor saw Bob, he held her up. "Meet Karen Sue!" he said, beaming.

When settled at home, Bob and I began praying in thanksgiving at Karen's crib each night. This began a pattern of praying as a couple that has continued through the years. Another sanctuary of God's presence.

One day when Karen was about four months old, I drove past

St. Andrew's Church. I wanted to take her in but felt awkward about it. Yet before I knew it, we were out of the car. I carried her into the empty, still sanctuary.

I looked into Karen's little face as I held her to me. "This is where I talked to God," I whispered. "Here is where I prayed to be able to have a baby." My throat tightened and I choked out more words. "You see, God in all His love, heard me. He gave us you!" I kissed her cheek and with blurred eyes I looked at that same gold cross on the altar. "Thank You, O Lord, thank You! I praise You!"

As I ponder these answered prayers, I know God, in His wisdom, doesn't always give believers everything they want. But He does act in our lives in sovereign ways.

Two years after Karen's arrival, I gave birth to our son, John. Again, Bob and I were thrilled at God's gift.

My "secret sanctuary" at a church in Kansas City holds precious memories and God has provided many more secret sanctuaries in my spiritual journey over the years. A favorite one is the "together sanctuary" Bob and I have found every time we join in prayer. God provides abundant creative places for us to seek Him and to find Him—when we seek Him with our whole hearts.

The Day My Plate Was Broken

MAX LUCADO

t was past midnight in Dalton, Georgia, as I stood in a dimly lit phone booth making a call to my folks. My first summer job away from home wasn't panning out as it was supposed to. The work was hard. My two best friends had quit and gone back to Texas, and I was bunking in the Salvation Army until I could find an apartment.

For a big, tough nineteen-year-old, I sure felt small.

The voices of my mom and dad had never sounded so sweet. And although I tried to hide it; my loneliness was obvious. I had promised my parents that if they'd let me go, I'd stick it out for the whole summer. But now those three months looked like eternity.

As I explained my plight, I could tell my mom wanted me to come home. But just as she said, "Why don't you come . . .," my dad, who was on the extension, interrupted her. "We'd love for you to come back, but we've already broken your plate." (That was west Texas talk for "We love you, Max, but it's time to grow up.")

It takes a wise father to know when to push his son out of the nest. It's painful, but it has to be done. I'll always be thankful that my dad gave me wings and then made me use them.

Two War-Time Miracles

QUIN SHERRER

hen Marine Major General Charles Krulak needed a miracle of water for troops about to lead an attack on Iraq during the 1991 war in the Persian Gulf, he did what he always did—he prayed.

He had been assigned to prepare supplies for the frontal attack by allied forces against Iraqi troops. Because of a threat of chemical warfare, lots of water would be needed for the decontamination process.

He thought he was ready, having dug water wells that could supply one hundred thousand gallons a day for the ground offensive.

Then General Norman Schwarzkopf's strategy changed as the Iraqis dug in. General Krulak's operation was to move to a flat area called "gravel plains," seventy-four miles to the northwest.

As they dug for water there, only desert dust came out. The general consulted oil company engineers and Saudi bedouins. Still no water—only dry holes.

General Krulak prayed every day for a solution to the water problem as well as for the war effort. Ever since 1977 he had made it a practice to pray at 7:15 each morning. Staff members were invited to join him. The anticipated ground attack was only a few days away. One morning a colonel interrupted their prayer meeting to ask the general to accompany him somewhere. He had discovered something but he wouldn't say what. He wanted the general to see for himself.

As they traveled down a road built by the Marine Corps, they saw what looked like a pipe sticking out of the ground about fifty meters off the road. A bar protruding from the pipe formed a cross. Then the general saw at the base of the pipe a newly painted red pump, a green diesel generator, four new batteries still wrapped in plastic, and one thousand gallons of diesel fuel stored in a tank above the ground.

All the equipment was new, and everything seemed ready to

operate—except there was no key to start the generator. The general looked at his officer and said, "God did not put this here for us to be defeated for lack of a key."

Amazingly, when General Krulak pushed the starter, the new German-made generator purred and water began to flow. The well flowed within ten gallons of the one hundred thousand a day needed for the assault.

The general had traveled down that road many times, as had a division of men, some twenty thousand troops. No one had reported seeing that pipe.

General Krulak believes the well appeared as an answer to prayer. "There was no way anyone could have driven down that road and not seen that well and equipment painted in multiple colors. The United States Forces did not use diesel fuel; therefore, I believe the Lord provided fuel we did not have," he said.

Others thought the Saudis may have put the well there. "Even if the well had already been there, its discovery came at exactly the right time," General Krulak said.

With the water problem solved, military experts still predicted heavy casualties. Krulak believes God performed yet another miracle in answer to prayer. On February 24, just fifteen minutes before the 4 A.M. ground attack, the wind shifted, blowing from the southwest to northeast. Winds always blow in the same direction in that part of the country, Krulak said.

This change of wind neutralized the threat of poison gas, which now would have blown back toward the Iraqis. The wind changed back to its normal direction on February 28, within minutes of General Schwarzkopf's cease-fire order.

"That," declares Krulak, now the Commandant of the United States Marine Corps, "is the power of prayer."

One could call it a double miracle in the middle of a war.

Just Fifty Dollars

VERDA J. GLICK

 don't know how much longer I can take care of all these sick people in my kitchen, Eli. This room becomes so small so fast," I told my husband. I had just ushered the last patient to the door. Now I rinsed hypodermic syringes and put them in a pan to boil. I lined up the containers of gauze, tape, and cotton on the little table beside the refrigerator and covered it with a clean cloth.

My husband remarked, "Ever since the natives found out you're a nurse, they've kept you busy."

"Oh, but I love it. Anyway, that's why we came to El Salvador, to serve, right?"

"Right. You certainly have plenty of opportunities. It seems like more come every day."

"Yes, besides those who come for vitamin shots, many come for first aid. Yesterday I treated a child who scalded himself with hot coffee. Today a man came with a machete slash."

"What you need is a little clinic in the backyard," Eli said.

"I think you're right," I agreed. I opened the refrigerator to look for something for lunch. "That would be much better than having sick people traipsing through our house. I hate to think of the germs they bring with them. But what about the money? How much would a little building cost?"

"Oh, I think I could build a little shack for about fifty dollars."

"Do you think God wants us to have a clinic?"

"Well," Eli answered, "We can find out. Let's pray and ask God to send us fifty dollars if He wants us to build a clinic."

Eli and I knelt. Almost hesitantly we prayed, "Dear Lord, if it is Your will for us to build a clinic, please send us fifty dollars."

Several days later, we received a letter. When we opened it, a fifty-dollar check fell out. It had been written before we prayed.

In the abundance of funds we received in the weeks that followed, God showed us that He is capable of giving us much more than fifty dollars. Eli built, not a little shack, but a two-room complex. We had enough money left to buy an examining table, a dentist chair, a small refrigerator, and all the medical equipment we needed.

That happened more than thirty years ago. Thirty-two thousand Salvadorans have received treatment in Clinica Cristana since that first wavering prayer. Now whenever we need something, Eli and I turn to the Great Provider Who showed us that He can give us much more than just fifty dollars.

She Made Footprints

LEE HILL-NELSON

y sisters and I sat on our front porch eating after-school snacks. In the far distance, a familiar figure dressed in white trudged down the dusty road leading from the school house. We wondered who Mrs. Molly Reese, my fourth grade teacher, would visit today.

Mrs. Reese taught third, fourth, and fifth grades, all in one room, in the Bridle Bit School in the Texas Panhandle. It was not unusual to see her make home visits after school. What was unusual, is she walked everywhere she went. She was a widow and had no car. I thought she was at least one hundred years old. Today I'd guess she was sixty.

I can see her now. White hair framed her gentle, wrinkled face. Some folks described her as being stout. Others said she was heavy on her feet.

It was a typical west Texas spring day, warm and sunny, a bit of dust blowing with whirlwinds popping up here and yonder.

As she rounded the last bend in the road, we knew she was coming to our house.

Did I do something wrong at school today? I wondered.

She climbed the wooden steps to our porch, short of breath and perspiring. Her hand touched my shoulder and she said, "It's going to be all right. May I speak to your father?"

Papa looked surprised when he saw her on the porch. She stood there smiling a sweet smile, looking up at this tall, handsome, dark-skinned man with a stoic personality, daring to confront him—something I was afraid to do.

A decayed tooth with an abscess on my gum was causing me pain at school and Mrs. Reese didn't like that. Mama "doctored" it the best she could with cloves spice and by placing a heated wash cloth on my jaw. But Papa wouldn't relent and take me to a dentist because he said, "It'd be a waste of money."

Papa was one of three trustees for the school district and had a vote on hiring teachers. As I stood and listened, I wondered how

139

Mrs. Reese could be so brave and risk her job. With her quiet manner, she told Papa that the toothaches interrupted my schoolwork and that taking care of teeth when children are young was very important.

At first, Papa seemed angry. But then he gradually relaxed. Whether from embarrassment or from her gentle persuasion, he promised to take me to the dentist on Saturday.

Mrs. Reese stayed a while to chat, then said goodbye to Papa and me. She headed toward the setting sun, back to the school teachers' house for a night's rest. Her day's work ended, her mission was accomplished.

She was more than a teacher. She made footprints on the dusty roads she walked, but more important, she made footprints on her students' lives. She taught reading, writing, and arithmetic, but she also taught the importance of abundantly caring.

Faithfulness

Because God is faithful, we know He'll come through for us—even if it's at the last moment. He wants us to be just as dependable as we represent Him to others. A promise is a promise; God always keeps His promises.

I do not hide your righteousness in my heart;
I speak of your faithfulness and salvation.
I do not conceal your love and your truth
from the great assembly.

PSALM 40:10 (NIV)

My God's Financial
Restoration Program

ELLEN BERGH

eaving the store with an armload of groceries, I glanced at my elderly mother and before I knew what I was saying, I told her, "God is going to restore the years the locusts ate of your life."

Old-country Irish, Mom had taken a dim view of our coming to Christ in our thirties. Now she looked at me with scorn. "And just how is He going to do all that?" she asked.

It was a good question. She'd worked hard all her life, making low wages in spite of her bright intellect. She'd single-parented two girls and had no assets for her old age. Her future did look bleak. All I could say was that I sensed His promise. A month later, mom almost got mugged catching a bus to work in Los Angeles. We prayed harder for God's protection around her and for the fulfillment of His promise.

No wonder Mom was skeptical. Our own finances reminded me of a junkyard. Relics of broken dreams and debts littered the landscape. Instead of passing a fairy wand over it all, God prompted me to clean it up one clunker problem at a time. I began to reconstruct seven years of overdue tax returns, a task so daunting, I almost shrank from doing it.

Each day after prayer, I set the kitchen timer to tackle the depressing carnage fifteen minutes at a time. I sorted through receipts, pay stubs and documentation about a tax boondoggle dating to time overseas. *Didn't I help my husband out of similar situations before we became Christians? If I fix this, won't it all just happen again?* I wondered bitterly. *But we need to come clean to the Internal Revenue Service and stop living in fear of reprisals.* Mother voiced worry that we might be convicted of tax evasion. A Christian friend who was an accountant looked over my seven years worth of forms along with our letter of apology, and warned me I was admitting too much liability. Yet I felt God wanted me to tell the whole truth.

The day came when I hand-carried the forms to the IRS with my letter of apology. We had thrown ourselves on the mercy of God and waited for the tidal wave of penalties that could capsize our finances. When the IRS audited the returns, refunds due from some of the past offset other penalties we owed. We paid an amount far lower than what we'd expected and were free of that yoke of worry. We were thrilled and praised God!

When I reported the outcome to Mother she didn't say much. Two months later she called and jubilantly said, "Watching you face that mess gave me the courage to file for my Social Security. Though I'd paid for forty-five years since immigrating from Ireland, I'd worried whether I was entitled. Social Security just sent me a retroactive settlement of all I should have collected since I turned 65!"

With her windfall and help from my sister, Mom bought a home in Portland, Oregon. Within days of moving in, she inherited a house full of furniture my brother-in-law had kept in storage since his mother's death. God continued His abundant restoration in her with an unexpected blessing of another granddaughter the year she turned 71.

God has been faithful to the message He gave me at the grocery store about my mother's future—and my own. Years have gone by, and we haven't had to hide from the IRS again. What God restores is permanent.

Abundant Wisdom

JEAN ANN DUCKWORTH

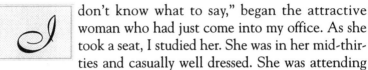 don't know what to say," began the attractive woman who had just come into my office. As she took a seat, I studied her. She was in her mid-thirties and casually well dressed. She was attending the women's conference at my church. One of the services offered during the conference was counseling appointments with the pastoral staff. As a pastoral intern at the church, I was asked to handle a portion of the appointments. I must admit, I was nervous about the whole thing. As a third-year seminary student, working toward my Master of Divinity, I was required to do a church internship. However, I had realized the year before that I was not called to pastoral ministry.

As such, I felt myself ill equipped to face the challenges set before me during my internship. Worst of these challenges were the counseling sessions. Each time, I would take a deep breath, send up a silent prayer, and press on. This time was no exception. I experienced even more self-doubt when the woman before me explained that she herself was a trained therapist She had not been able to help herself and she hoped I might be able to give her some guidance. With a very strong prayer for help, I settled down to listen to her story.

I was not prepared for the painful tale she related to me. Three years earlier, she and her husband were overwhelmed when, upon the birth of their first child, they were told he would not live more than a few hours. He suffered from a hereditary disease. There was nothing the doctors could do. During the short hours that followed, she and her husband held and cuddled the dying child until he passed on. Life went on and eventually they found they were to be parents again. Doctors performed tests during her pregnancy. The news they had for the couple was not good. Their second child, again a son, appeared to have the same disease. The doctors recommended terminating the pregnancy. Instead, she and her husband decided to pray for a miracle. The day came when their son was born. The miracle they had prayed for did not occur and again they lost a child within hours of birth.

I was amazed how calmly the woman related the details of both her sons' deaths. She did begin to show some emotion as she went on to explain how she knew she was the one from whom her sons inherited the disease. Her husband had two grown children from a previous marriage. No sign of the disease had appeared before in his family. She paused.

Looking at me, she asked, "Why won't God let me be a mother? I want children so badly. Why did He do this to me?" With that, the flood gate opened. Her anger came pouring out and, as she spoke, a shocking fact became very clear: she blamed Jesus for the deaths of her sons. She hated Him. She could not forgive Him for what He had done to her. Her anger was so great, she couldn't even bring herself to say His name. Finally, she calmed down, sat back, and looked at me expectantly.

The whole time she had been talking, my mind had been racing. I knew eventually she would finish speaking and expect me to say something. What was I going to say? I had no idea. So I sat silently for a moment as I prayed for divine guidance. Sensing nothing, I opened my mouth to speak and was stunned by the words that came out.

I told her to close her eyes. I then asked her to envision Jesus as she saw Him. "He is sitting in a chair," I told her. "Now picture Him sitting there holding your sons, one in each arm. Look at His face as He looks down at them. See the love and tenderness and care on His face. Now look at your sons' faces. See how happy they are. They're safe and they're loved and they know it. They love Him and know He cares for them."

She had begun to quietly cry. "God isn't saying you can never be a mother. You just may never be a mother in this life. Instead, you will be their mother for an eternity. In the meantime, Jesus will take care of them for you. Do you see that?"

She nodded and began crying harder. I got on my knees on the floor in front of her chair. She fell into my arms. "Let go. They don't belong to you anymore."

The poor woman began sobbing as I held her there. For five minutes, she cried until she could cry no more. I knew I had broken through her anger. The next few minutes were spent pulling ourselves back together.

As she prepared to leave the office, she stopped and turned to me. "Remember how I said I didn't know what to say?"

I nodded.

"What I wanted to say was, 'Help me let go of my sons.' I just could not bring myself to say it. I thought you should know."

As she closed the door behind her, I sat there with tears in my eyes. Once again, the Lord had given me the abundant gifts I needed when I needed them.

Rubber Bands Galore

KATHY COLLARD MILLER

athy, where are some more rubber bands? There aren't enough to go around," Deborah said.

I'd asked Deborah to help me distribute rubber bands at the end of the rows of chairs at the retreat center. Now she was standing at my side, looking expectantly at me. Most of the women were out on the coffee break before the next session was scheduled to start and I wanted each one of them to have a rubber band. But I didn't have any more. "I thought I brought enough, but I guess not," I answered, feeling disappointed.

When I speak at retreats, I often pass out a rubber band to each woman to put on her wrist. I explain, "When you notice that you are speaking negatively about yourself, snap your rubber band. And if you hear someone else here during the weekend talk negatively about herself, snap her rubber band!" Usually, everyone moans or claps depending upon who their friends are!

I continue by explaining, "This way you'll learn the principle of Second Corinthians 10:5 which says to 'take every thought captive to the obedience of Christ.'"

But now all the women wouldn't be able to take part in the project. *Oh, Lord, why didn't I plan sufficiently?* I felt like snapping a rubber band on my wrist right then!

As I began to turn away, one of the attendees walked up to me and said, "Did I hear you talking about needing rubber bands?"

I nodded.

"I just happened to look outside the conference room at that clump of trees and there are lots of rubber bands scattered on the ground."

Scattered on the ground? I couldn't believe it. We were at a Christian conference center located in the mountains. Why would rubber bands be scattered on the ground?

Deborah and I quickly went to the tree the woman pointed out and sure enough! There were rubber bands scattered on the ground—more than enough to make up for what I lacked. I rejoiced as we picked them up, flicked off the dirt and began to place them at the end of the rows. Everyone would wear a rubber band after all! *Lord, thank you for your abundant provision of rubber bands!*

Now, how did the Lord know I would need more of them and who did He use to put them there?

A Surprise Ending

CAROL KENT

ne day Dad was visiting parishioners in the local hospital. He stopped in a room unexpectedly and met Francis Kent. Dad sensed that Francis was hungry for spiritual meaning in his life and decided to meet with him at a later date. A few weeks passed and Francis was released from the hospital.

On New Year's Day my father thought about this man again and asked if I would baby-sit while he and Mother visited Francis and his family. Baby-sitting was not my favorite activity. Grudgingly, I agreed to baby-sit my four younger sisters and my brother while Mom and Dad visited with the Kents.

After they arrived, Mom and Dad sat around a little kitchen table and shared the plan of salvation with Francis and his wife. Just as they were about to invite Christ into their lives, their seventeen-year-old son stuck his head around the corner. He hesitantly said, "I'm sorry for interrupting, but I've been listening in on this conversation, and I wonder if I could become a Christian, too." That night young Gene Kent joined his parents in prayer and made the decision to make Christ the center of his life.

When Mom and Dad got home and told me that Gene Kent had just become a Christian, I GOT EXCITED! For several years my father had been announcing, "There will be absolutely no dating of non-Christians for my five daughters!" That was a problem. We lived in a very small town, and we were in a very small church. At that point there were eight girls in the church youth group—and only two guys. One of them was so unattractive you prayed he wouldn't ask you to go out on a date. And the other one was so "drop-dead gorgeous" you could get killed in the stampede of women running after his admiring glance. I couldn't believe there was now a third possibility in the form of handsome, dynamic, intelligent Gene Kent!

That day, while I was at home doing the mundane, ordinary,

not-very-much-loved job of baby-sitting and nothing exceptional seemed to be happening in my life, my mother and father were out winning my future husband to Jesus Christ! And from that day to this I've discovered some of God's best surprises happen on my *daily* days.

A Treasured Legacy

CHARLES R. SWINDOLL

hen I completed my own study of the letter to the Philippians, I experienced a nostalgic serendipity. As I was putting away my research materials along with pen and paper, an old book by F. B. Meyer, one of my favorite authors, caught my attention. It happened to be his work on Philippians, but I had not consulted it throughout my months of study.

Thinking there might be something in it to augment my study, I decided to pull it from the shelf and leaf through it before I went home for the day. I turned off the overhead light in my study, and, with only the light from my desk lamp, I leaned back in my old leather desk chair and opened Meyer's book.

To my unexpected delight, it was not the words of F. B. Meyer that spoke to me that evening, but the words of my mother. For as I began looking through it, I realized this book was one of the many volumes which had found their way from her library into mine after her death back in 1971. Little did she know when she wrote in it years before that her words would become a part of her legacy to me, her youngest. I sat very still as I took in the wonder.

In her own inimitable handwriting, my mother had made notes in the text and along the margins throughout the book. When I got to the end, I noticed she had penned these words on the inside of the back cover, "Finished reading this May 8, 1958."

I looked up in my dimly lit study and pondered 1958. My mind took me back to a tiny island in the South Pacific where I had spent many lonely months as a Marine. I recalled that it was in May of 1958 that I had reached a crossroad in my own pilgrimage. In fact, I had entered the following words in my journal: "The Lord has convinced me that I am to be in His service. I will begin to make plans to prepare for a lifetime of ministry." Amazingly, it was in the same month of that very year that my mother had finished reading Meyer's book. As I looked back over the pages, I found one reference after another to her prayers for me as

I was away . . . her concern for my spiritual welfare . . . her desire for God's best in my life. And occasionally she had inserted a clever quip or humorous comment.

Turning back to the front of the book, I found another interesting entry, also with a date. It read, "Chart of Philippians mailed to me by Charles when he was ministering in Massachusetts, 1966." As I glanced over the chart, another memory swept over me. I recalled putting that chart together and sending it to her during my years in New England. Once again I looked up and momentarily relived those years between 1958 and 1966. What a significant passage! All through that time, I now realize my mother had prayed for me and loved me and sought God's best for me.

Across the room in my study hangs an original oil painting with a light above it, shedding a golden glow down over the colorful canvas. The painting was my mother's gift to me some years after I entered the ministry. She had painted it. It is of a shepherd surrounded by a handful of sheep on a green hillside.

I had looked at this painting countless times before, but this time was unique. In the bottom right corner I looked at her name and the date . . . only days before she passed into the Lord's presence. Caught in that nostalgic time warp, I turned off my desk lamp and stared at the lighted painting. There I sat, twenty years after she had laid the brush aside, thanking God anew for my mother's prayers, my pilgrimage, and especially His presence. Faithfully, graciously, quietly He had led me and helped me and blessed me. I bowed my head and thanked Him for His sustaining grace . . . and I wept with gratitude.

Suddenly the shrill sound of the telephone broke the silence. My younger son, Chuck, was on the line wanting to tell me something funny that had happened. I quickly switched gears and enjoyed one of those delightful, lighthearted father-son moments. As we laughed loudly together, he urged me to hurry home.

Following his call I placed the F. B. Meyer book back on the shelf. As I was leaving my study, I paused beside the painting and thought of the significant role my parents had played in those formative years of my life . . . and how the torch had been passed on from them to Cynthia and me to do the same with our sons and daughters . . . and they, in turn, with theirs.

As I switched off the light above the painting, I smiled and said, "Good-bye, Mother." In the darkness of that room I could almost hear her voice answering me, "Good-bye, Charles. I love you, Son. I'm still praying for you. Keep walking with God . . . and don't forget to have some fun with your family tonight."

What a treasured legacy: devoted prayers, lasting love, hearty laughter. That's the way it ought to be.

Bringing God to Work

RUDY GALDONIK

s I walked into the travel agency for the first time as an owner—with only eighteen weeks of training under my belt—I wondered how I was going to do it. If there was one thing I learned in Travel School, it was that I didn't know much of anything at all. The gentleman who was now my new partner introduced me to our two full-time agents and showed me my desk. I smiled cordially, hoping they wouldn't notice my trembling hands.

As I sat down at the empty desk, I did something that seemed to come naturally in times of crisis. I prayed—not an elegant or particularly profound prayer—probably more like, "God, I don't have a clue what I'm doing, so I'm giving this business to You." Little did I know, as the weeks grew to months, I would think back on that prayer many times as I began to see what I'd gotten myself into.

The first thing that didn't make sense was that the phones never rang. With seven lines coming into the agency, there was an eerie silence during most of the day. And then one day I had the opportunity to pick up the mail. As I slowly walked back to the office, I began to open the stack of letters. Most of the correspondence threatened my partner, "You better pay up or else."

I laid the mail out on my partner's desk and asked, "What gives?"

He slumped over the desk and began to shake. As I starred with my mouth hanging open, he painted a picture of debt and financial loss; a completely different picture than what my husband and I had heard from him when we considered buying into the agency only a few months earlier. I was shocked, devastated and terrified of what this all meant.

The following Friday, the staff announced that they were not returning to work the following Monday. They were sick and tired of the games and lies of my partner. Without them, there would be no recourse but to close the business.

I called my husband at his office and told him to come to my office in an hour for an emergency staff meeting. I had one last airline ticket to deliver and as I drove I started to cry. As a distraction, I decided to turn on the radio. It was tuned to a Christian station. A man just finished his program and said, "Just remember that today's challenges and crises are tomorrow's credentials" and then the station returned to music.

I stared at the radio and blinked back tears. "Lord, you're reminding me of that very first day when I prayed, aren't You? I turned the business over to You and I'm not going to take it back. I just need to trust You."

When I returned to the office, my husband and I shared for the first time with the staff who we were and what was important in our lives. We agreed the agency needed a lot of hard work, but we promised that we would be there to see it through if they would help us. The staff stayed.

Since the trust was broken between my partner and me, there was no hope for us to work successfully together. I offered to buy his half of the agency and he accepted.

The next task was to create a business where only a shell of one existed. Expenses were cut to the bare bones. We spent money to improve customer service. As time went on, we relied on the expertise of our staff to identify ways to bring in new business and we watched their excitement as the phones began to ring. Existing clients saw the change and started to make referrals for new business.

In His faithfulness, God placed unbelievable opportunities in my lap. One day, I tried calling an organization but didn't know I'd been given a wrong number by mistake. I called and said, "Hi, I'm a travel agent."

The person answering the phone gasped and said, "I need a travel agent! I'm responsible for an international sports tournament this coming summer and I need an agency to handle the travel plans." In time, our agency was selected and because of that opportunity, we opened a whole new division with a sports marketing focus one year later.

As God continued to bless my business, we moved to larger, nicer offices. Many times, the original two agents and I have reminisced about how it was in the early days. And I remembered that prayer on my very first day. When it looked like all was lost, God told me that "today's challenges and crises are tomorrows credentials."

College Bound

GOLDEN KEYES PARSONS

 buried my face in my pillow to muffle the sounds of sobbing. There was no place to be alone in our tiny apartment. I was the oldest child of an alcoholic father. My mother did her best to keep the family together and worked hard to pay the bills. It seemed, however, there was never enough to go around. My parents separated during my senior year in high school. My mom, my younger brother, and I moved into a small, one-bedroom duplex that summer. I was a cheerleader and an honor student, active in several clubs, the school choral group, and church. But we had no car, so I was constantly having to find rides to get everywhere.

All of these circumstances were hard, but the most difficult was the fact there was no prospect of college. As I buried my face in that pillow, I prayed, "Oh, God. Is there any way for me to go to college? Please make a way for me."

"Where are you going to college?" my choral teacher asked. I mumbled something about no money being available for college. This particular teacher had taken an interest in me the past couple of years and was aware of the problems I faced. She was a "Mr. Holland" (as in *Mr. Holland's Opus*) in my life.

"Well, if you were going, where would you like to go?" she asked.

"Oh, Baylor University! That's where I want to go. That's where the Lord wants me to go."

"Oh, yeah? Baylor? That's a pretty expensive school."

"I know. That's why I can't go, but if I could afford to go, that's the place for me."

Baylor University is a Christian university in Waco, TX. From the moment I accepted the Lord as a teenager, I felt a call on my life to go into the ministry. I wanted to go to a Christian college and prepare for whatever role the Lord had for me. Our youth minister had taken the youth group to Baylor for a football game and I fell in love with it. I knew that was where the

Lord wanted me. I just didn't know how He was going to work out this miracle.

My mom kept telling me there was no way I could go. Just like there was no way I could be a cheerleader, or go on such and such trip, or whatever. Every time such a situation arose I would tell her, "If the Lord wants me to do that or go there, He will work it out. You don't worry about it . . . just sit back and watch what He does." And He always provided.

But this was a big order. Could He really do something *this* big? Hardly anyone received scholarships then and I didn't think I could qualify for the few that were available. Would God do the impossible for *me*? My faith was wavering.

One afternoon late in the school year, the school counselor, who was also a deacon in my church, called me to his office. It was the first time I had ever been called to the office! I could not imagine why. Had I done something wrong? The afternoon sun streamed through the venetian blinds in his office, spilling onto his desk, seeming to tease me with its joy.

"Golden, I have not seen any college applications for you come across my desk. Why not?"

"Mr. Smith, I cannot afford to go to college."

"If you could go, where would you like to go?"

I gulped and bravely replied, "Baylor University."

The next thing I knew I was scheduled to go to Waco and take a battery of tests to see if I qualified for any scholarships. I rode a bus to the small town by myself. I honestly do not remember how I got from the bus station to the campus, but I did make it for my appointment with the vice-president of the university. I was escorted all around campus by a beautiful young student . . . whom I found out later was a wonderful Christian girl and a Baylor Beauty.

The next fall God did the impossible! I rejoiced as I entered Baylor University as a freshman. God's provision was complete all the way down the line . . . a scholarship and a job in the office of the president of the university. The women's missionary organization at my church bought new glasses for me. My Sunday School teacher loaded me up in her car and helped move me into the dormitory.

As I stood on the fourth floor of the freshman dorm, watching her and my mom drive off, I felt very alone—but only for a moment. I knew deep in my spirit God had provided for me to be in this place and He would continue to abundantly provide for all my needs.

The Amputee

ARLENE CENTERWALL

t was one o' clock in the morning and I was a night nurse in a community hospital in Montreal in 1977. One of my patients was Jim—a motorcycle type and an above-the-knee amputee. When I approached him about his narcotic order, I sensed his anger. *Problems again*, I lamented. Tonight I didn't feel like an angel in white as my heart hardened toward him. I shined the flashlight on the covers of his bed and he bolted upright barking, "Give me my pain killer *now!*"

"I'm sorry, Jim, you can't have it until three o'clock," I answered as gently as I could, trying to quell the quaking of my voice. "Your order says that you can have it every four hours and it's only been three hours since you received it. I'll bring it to you as soon as you're allowed to have it."

"You blankety blank nurse. Give me the stuff or I'll . . . I'll get you. . . . I have friends, you know. . . . I'm getting out of here! Now!"

I shuddered when I thought about his motorcycle gang.

I shut my ears to his piercing screams as I left to continue my rounds. Lately it felt as though I was the only one holding up a standard. Nurses on other shifts caved in to Jim, giving him whatever he wanted whenever he wanted it. He was becoming addicted to his narcotic. The surgeon had left an order in the order book that Jim could have the narcotic "every 4 hours only." The order was written in letters two inches high so I knew that the surgeon meant business. But when Jim shouted and acted out, others would simply call the intern who shrugged and gave his consent.

It had been three weeks since Jim's surgery and his pain should not have been as severe as he insisted. Besides he didn't display any of the classic signs of real pain.

I raced around the frantic ward, trying to meet patients' needs. *I don't need this*, I sighed. I saw Jim getting out of bed and laboriously hopping to the corridor on one leg. Slowly he let himself down and began dragging himself on his bottom toward the desk. He was as dramatic as he could be. I peered at him from the corner of my eye. Visions of his motorcycle gang flashed before me.

I felt like quitting. *Another terrible night*, I sighed. *Lately everything seems so frantic and psychiatric problems compound the stress. Why do these confrontations always happen to me? I don't have time for this nonsense. I'll pretend not to notice him.* I hurried down the hall.

As a Christian, I knew I should do the right thing but it was taking a toll on my emotions. Others seemed to capitulate to his demands so easily but that caused him to become accustomed to the drugs.

I thought, *It would be so much easier just to give in, call the intern and ask for a repeat on the order. He'll give it because he doesn't want to be bothered. After all, it won't be our problem in several days when he's discharged.*

"Oh, Lord, I'm getting so tired of this. Please strengthen me," I whispered under my breath at those times. And He did, over and over again, regardless of how hard it was or how much I knew Jim would verbally abuse me.

Because he was in the end room, it took Jim some time to shuffle up to the desk. It would have been amusing if it was not so tragic. The door to the ward whooshed open. The supervisor swished to the desk and looked quizzically at Jim.

"What's going on here?" she asked quietly.

"Trust me in this . . . he wants his Demerol too soon," I explained.

She nodded and ignored him as she took a report from me.

When she left, Jim arrived at the desk. Beads of perspiration dotted his forehead.

"You'll have to sign these 'refusal of treatment forms' before you go," I said, handing him the forms. "And here's the phone . . . you'll need to call someone to come pick you up."

He sat there staring ahead of him. Then it happened. Suddenly he burst into tears, sobbing uncontrollably. Surprised, I let him weep for several minutes. I melted. When it was over, I lowered myself to his level and said:

Gentleness

$\mathscr{A}$ gentle touch or a gentle response can be soothing in a time of distress. God's words to us are always gentle for He understands our struggles. Can we not give the same kind of gentle encouragement to others?

Let your gentleness be evident to all.
The Lord is near.

PHILIPPIANS 4:5 (NIV)

Footprints

LAURA SABIN RILEY

e trudged along the dirt path, kicking up dust clouds and humming as we blazed a trail through the thick, colorful forest. God's creation was alive and beautiful; I admired the rich green of the pines and the bright purples and yellows of the wildflowers. My eyes then shifted to another of God's greatest creations directly in front of me.

His blonde hair glistened in the sunshine as he marched forward. His boots left small, but deep, tracks, as he pressed onward. "Look, Mom." Seth pointed at the ground. "There's my footprint! It means I've been there, huh?"

I smiled and nodded as my thoughts drifted with Seth's words. I had been discouraged the past few months, wondering if I was leaving any proof on his heart that I had "been there." Training Seth in godly character was a priority for me, but one that seemed to become increasingly difficult as he grew older. Simple Bible stories and quiet craft projects at the kitchen table on Tuesday afternoons didn't seem to be working anymore. "What does he need?" I had silently wondered. "How can I best impress God's commandments on his heart?" I was at a loss for keeping him interested in God. He was five, on the move, and into "fun." I desperately wanted him to understand that being a Christian *is* fun. But how? I sent up a desperate plea for wisdom.

Seth's sudden fire of questions broke my reverie. "Hey, Mom did you know that when you sin, you have to kill an animal? And did you know that no one really knows where the Garden of Eden is today? Oh yeah—and Satan is a fallen angel. Did you know that?"

He took a breath and looking behind him, smiled triumphantly, never missing a beat as he stomped forward.

Seth's spontaneous interest in spiritual matters stunned and delighted me. I was suddenly struck with the thought of Deuteronomy 6:6–7: "These commandments that I give you today are to be upon your hearts. Impress them on your children.

Talk about them when you sit at home and when you walk along the road, when you lie down and when you get up" (NIV).

"That's it!" I laughed as I realized God had chosen to answer my prayer and solve my dilemma in this exact moment.

"When you walk along the road," I pondered aloud, eyes stretched to scan the rocky mountain trail. I shuddered at the thought of the various times that Seth had shown interest in spiritual matters and I had brushed him off because I was busy doing something else or I was tired. I would reply to his questions with a harried, "We'll talk later, honey, when we have more time." But "later" never came because when I found the time to talk, Seth was no longer interested.

I sighed deeply, beginning to understand that I could no longer choose the opportunities to teach Seth what it means to follow Christ. If I wanted to be successful at leaving my footprints on the heart of my active little boy, then I had to watch for and seize the teachable moments as they appeared. Those were the moments when Seth was most interested in learning about God—like right now!

I breathed a prayer of thanks to the Lord for guiding me. Feeling a stab of remorse for the moments I had missed in the past, I pledged myself to becoming more alert so as not to miss many more. And there would be more—Seth was still young and very teachable.

Determined not to miss *this* moment, I quickened my pace to catch up with my son, leaving deep imprints in the dirt behind me.

Run After Him

JAN FRANK

ast summer, our family traveled to Hawaii. About four or five days into the vacation, I noticed that Don and I were on very different schedules. He arose early and got in his morning walk, while the girls and I slept in. Just about the time he came back to the room, I was heading out the door to do my morning devotional, poolside. After completing my devotions and prayer time, I went back to the room as Don was coming out to get some morning sun. As I came out to join him, he was off with the girls for a morning swim in the ocean, and so forth.

The Holy Spirit said to me, "If you do not do something to help cultivate your relationship, this is what it will be like once your daughters have left home." This stopped me in my tracks. As a marriage counselor, I saw many relationships where couples had seemed to drift apart over time. Even though Don and I were not fighting or upset with each other, we were not finding ways to nurture our relationship. Without saying a word to him, I agreed to a morning ocean swim, even though I was not that excited about giving up "my" morning. Later that day, Don volunteered to accompany me shopping, which is not his most favorite activity.

Later on that evening, Don asked me to go with him down to the water's edge and watch the sunset. At first I thought, "I'd rather finish the book that I've been reading," but I'm glad I didn't. I can still picture in my mind's eye that beautifully framed sunset, with the pinks, blues, and yellows painted across the sky. The glistening water splashed on the black volcanic rock, and the slight tropical breeze blew in the palms overhead. Lying on a lounge, we embraced one another, gazing silently at the scene. Don leaned over to pick up the camera, and my body naturally leaned with him as I was enfolded in his arms. Just that moment, the Spirit of God seemed to say, "This is what I want you to experience with me—an intimacy and closeness in which there is no need to concern yourself about the direction in which I am leading. I want you to lean into me, to be so close to my heart that you will naturally follow me, as you have just done with Don."

Had I not chosen to view a sunset, I might never have known the joy of such an intimate encounter—both with my husband and with God.

Hungry for God

WELLINGTON BOONE

 remember being in Nashville with some country western singers. There were about twenty-five of us in a room. With me was a good friend, Ricky Skaggs. What a heart he has for God. Meeting with us were two older gentlemen, much like patriarchs in the faith. They came to pray for us and to pass their mantles of faithfulness on to men younger in the Lord. While one of the men was praying over us, it became clear to me that everything he was praying for related directly to me and my needs. I knew it was a corporate prayer, but God was speaking every word to me.

When he finished, Ricky raised his hand and said, "You know, brother, while you were praying for those other guys, it was as if everything you were praying for these other people was mine."

I thought to myself, this guy is trying to be as greedy and hungry for God as I am! I immediately put my hand up and said, "Me, too. I felt the same thing." I was moved by Ricky's heart toward the Lord, and from that point on I was aware he was trying to "outhunger" me. I was not about to let another man be greedier for Jesus than I was! I had to keep an eye on him!

The inspiration of this country western singer gripped my heart. So genuine was his love for God—a true portrait of selflessness. I was determined to be part of this picture. Sometimes people think prominent people who have won the world's praise are more into money and people than seeking the applause of heaven. While this may be true of others it is certainly not true of Ricky.

The second gentleman gave a word, but noted he felt it was not necessary to pray over us. For a time he shared from his heart and imparted to us Godly wisdom. Suddenly Ricky got up, and the sound of water filling a basin could be heard. Before I knew it, he came around to this man and asked if he could wash his feet. With great dignity, the man took off his shoes, and Ricky quietly began the task. But he only washed one foot because I sprinted for the other one! Ricky was not going to be more humble for God than me. No sir! In a spirit of deep worship we became competitive for God—jealous over who would outserve the other in honoring this dear man. At this point another man joined us and began drying the man's feet. I'm sure this scene caused our God to smile. There we were, grown men, arguing over the feet of one of His saints!

Ricky then took the water away, but I got to put the shoes back on and tie the laces. I recalled the servant heart of Jesus and remembered how He washed the feet of His disciples and His admonition that we should wash one another's feet. Observing this kindly man of God I thought, how beautiful are the feet of them that preach the gospel of peace.

Another significant event transpired after the foot washing. The man of God felt refreshed, and he had it in his heart to pray for us and to lay hands on those of us who washed his feet. For a simple act, we had become recipients of his prayer.

The transference of anointing is seen from Elijah to Elisha, Moses to the seventy, and Paul to Timothy. We got some of that! Yes sir! But do you know what? I'm still hungry for more, for everything God has in store for me.

A Young Girl's Wish

JANIE NESS

y eyes narrowed as I leapt from the stairs into our living room and rushed toward six large presents, each as big as a single mattress. On the silver package trimmed with red bows was my name. I tossed a glance at the other packages under our tree and then spun my head back to savor this moment like cotton candy melting on the roof of my mouth.

That Christmas Eve night, 1964, I snuggled beside my brothers and sisters along the bricks in front of the crackling fire, awaiting the kick-off. Dad sat on his three-legged stool by the crowded tree, ready to distribute the gifts. Grandma and Grandpa, who had arrived two days earlier, were settled on the couch, next to Mom.

Staring at the glimmering twelve-foot Douglas fir, I recalled the six of us hiking to the forest behind our home, where we spent endless summer hours swimming and fishing in Pauly's Pond, to find our tree. As the youngest, I danced across the snow in the golden sunlight as the others towed our treasure home for presentation.

My mind lingered on the big silvery present, hoping my wish was inside. But Mom's words in early December hung like a shadow. "Money is especially tight this year."

After we opened the gifts under the tree, Dad stretched.

Anxious eyes watched his every move. "Are you ready for the big one?" he teased.

Smiling nervously, I rubbed my damp palms together.

"Okay, go find your name!" The sparkle in his eyes shined like a new penny. He loved giving. "When I say go, rip into it."

We flew to our prize, placed our fingers on the paper, resisting the urge to begin.

"Merry Christmas, kids. We hope you have lots of fun with these," Dad said, his voice quivering. "Enough said . . . Go!"

My hands fumbled as I pulled at the strips of paper.

"A bike!" someone screamed.

"Oh! Oh! A bike!" said another.

My brother, fifteen, and the oldest, shouted, "A four-ten shot-gun!"

My heart throbbed! *Is there enough money for all of us?* Then, I saw it! A picture of a bike on the cardboard box! Now, I could learn to ride. I leaned against the box, closing my eyes. "Oh, thank you, God," I whispered to someone I had barely met.

My limited knowledge of God was a week-long daily Bible School from the previous summer at the Grange Hall next door. My Popsicle-stick frame I crafted that held a picture of Jesus was kept under my bed with the other valued keepsakes of a seven-year-old, including the tiny black Bible from the summer school.

I hopped through the mountain of wrapping paper to Mom and Dad and showered them with hugs of gratitude. Mom put a 78 album on the stereo and then quickly set a feast of snacks on the kitchen counter, including Grandma's homemade desserts.

After much laughter, eating, and admiring our gifts, Mom suggested we say good-night, reminding us of opening our stockings in the morning. I slipped on my new flannel nightgown and fell into bed. "How could they afford all those bikes?" I thought.

And then six words appeared mysteriously in my mind like a colorful rainbow does in the sky. *He shall supply all your needs.* The message faded and I curled up, dreaming of the moment I would glide on my new bike.

At 7:00 A.M. I heard whispers coming from the bunk beds. My two sisters slipped out of bed, motioning for me to follow. We dashed to the bricks, snatching our filled stockings from the mantle, and then hurried back to empty the contents on our covers.

Soon, Mom and Grandma were preparing a delicious breakfast. At the table, we drilled Dad as to when we could ride our new bikes.

He chuckled, "The store clerk offered to assemble them for free, but your Mother insisted the surprise would be better if they were wrapped in boxes." He took a bite of waffle, raised an eyebrow and looked at Grandpa. "Are you up to the task, Pop?"

Our kitchen floor became an assembly line. Five hours later, we each stood next to our trophy. In a line, we pushed them across the street to Mr. Haus' house who had generously offered his air compressor to fill our tires. When he saw the Christmas morning parade coming, he came down the steps of his farm house and asked, "Who's first?"

I did learn to ride my black and white bike, granting me confidence and many years of simple enjoyment. I never went to church throughout my childhood and there was no conversation about God, yet when I was alone, I would occasionally pull out that Bible, attempt to read it, and wonder who this God was.

At age 27, when I gave my heart to the Lord, it was then that I fully understood that God's abundance was with me always.

The Tale of the Frog

JUNE CERZA KOLF

We live on the high desert in California, where the wind is a frequent, unwelcome visitor. We were having an especially windy spring and I was feeling edgy and frazzled from the constant blowing. While I was fixing dinner, I looked out into the backyard and said to my husband, "I really need to get outdoors and water the plants. I'll brave the wind and go out after dinner."

After dinner, I headed for the back door and saw the trees swaying in the breeze. *On second thought, maybe it will be calmer tomorrow. The plants will just have to wait another day,* I said to myself.

I sat down and picked up a magazine, but I couldn't concentrate. I had a nagging feeling about watering my plants. Unable to ignore it any longer, I got up with a sigh, and announced, "I'm going to have to go outside and water those plants, after all!" My husband just smiled and shook his head.

As soon as I walked outside I noticed an unusual ripple pattern in the swimming pool. In addition to the white caps from the wind, there was a little circle of ripples. I leaned over for a closer look and spotted a frog with his legs pedaling frantically. There was no escape for him. The tiles were too slippery for him to climb up on and there was no ledge to hang onto. Oh my!

"Jack," I hollered, "come quick and save a frog." Out the door came my nice husband to the rescue. He scooped up the frog and put him in the empty lot next door.

As I went about my watering task I caught myself smiling. The nagging feeling about watering the plants had been for a specific reason. The reason was not the dry plants at all; it was about a frog that needed to be rescued.

If God cares that much about a little frog, how can I ever doubt that He will abundantly provide for me?

Butterflies, Rocks, and Opposites

TINA KRAUSE

ine, I'm leaving!" I yelled, slamming the door behind me. Fuming, I sat on the back deck stairs and glared across the yard.

"Lord, I've had it," I snarled. "We just aren't on the same wavelength."

Jim and I were young Christians attempting to work out the problems of a shaky marriage. We were complete opposites: I was flighty and emotional; Jim was silent and intense.

I read all of the latest books on marriage, but a *Total Woman* I was not. And Jim was less than the pastoral image with whom I had hoped to share my life.

My husband's lack of spiritual fervor concerned me. He was less evangelistic, less outwardly "spiritual" than I, which magnified the conflicts and widened the gap between us.

"How can two Christians who love You differ and argue so much?" I questioned. "And why can't Jim see how wrong he is?"

While mumbling my complaints to God, I noticed a brilliantly colored butterfly flutter past, dipping and swooping in all directions. At first its movements reminded me of my own. Anxiously, I had flittered in every direction busying myself in the "work of the Lord" while, from my perspective, Jim barely penetrated his spiritual cocoon.

Blinded to my husband's spiritual gifts, I pleaded with God in self-righteous tones. "Lord, stir Jim within and make him a powerhouse for You so that *both* of us can serve You together."

The monarch butterfly landed on a smooth, gray rock and, for a moment, rested. The sun's rays reflected off its stilled wings. This time its colors radiated more brightly than before as God silenced my sanctimonious thoughts.

"*You are a butterfly, but Jim is a rock,*" God whispered to my spirit. "*Rest on the abilities and wisdom I have imparted to him.*"

The Scripture from the Book of Corinthians suddenly came

alive: "There are different kinds of service, but the same Lord" (I Corinthians 12:5 NIV).

The air that soured with hostility moments before filled with the peace of the Holy Spirit. God grounded my butterfly wings on the spiritual head of my "rock" husband, and the healing began.

Twenty-three years later, our differences have transformed into an abundant ministry of appreciation for one another and a steadfast love. For that day, God began to teach me that my wedding vows include a mutual respect, admiration, and appreciation for rocks as well as butterflies.

Self-Control

Self-control must be the hardest thing in the world for us to achieve, yet God desires to develop it in us—even as we kick and scream! We may lack that important quality, but God has it in abundance. He never reacts inappropriately. Let's learn to do the same.

For this very reason, make every effort to add to your faith goodness; and to goodness, knowledge; and to knowledge, self-control; and to self-control, perseverance; and to perseverance, godliness; and to godliness, brotherly kindness; and to brotherly kindness, love.

2 Peter 1:5–7 (NIV)

A "Slick" Trick

JOAN RAWLINS BIGGAR

etting to the meeting at Becky's house that March day with my carload of passengers posed no problem, though the snowy road twisted up hills and plunged over ridges. Winter still gripped interior Alaska but a bright sun promised spring's return.

When we left hours later, Becky warned us all to keep our speed up until we topped the ridge opposite her rustic log home. The afternoon sun had warmed the ice enough to make it slick. The cars of other departing guests skidded and slipped across the narrow span of fill dirt which crossed the intervening gully. But I didn't worry. My heavy Checker Marathon, a passenger version of the original Checker cabs, could go where lighter vehicles stalled. We crossed the ravine easily and started up the hill.

We'd nearly reached the top when a man on a three-wheeler roared over the rise. There wasn't room for both vehicles. I slowed to avoid him. Our rear wheels began to spin. Though I tried to urge the car upward, it slid into a snowbank and stopped.

The three-wheeler drove on past while I eased the car backward around a curve and onto the fill. But something was wrong. The powerful engine ran so fast the wheels wouldn't quit turning on the ice. Every time I braked, the car skidded. Each attempt to slow backed us nearer the edge of the fill. Finally, at the very edge of the drop-off, I managed to bring the heavy vehicle to a stop. My frightened passengers stared into the tops of trees growing in the ravine below. They got out, while I remained in the car.

"We've got to pray," I gasped, and bowed my head. "Lord, please show us what to do."

Just like that, my hands knew the answer. They moved the gearshift into neutral and turned the wheel. The car responded perfectly. I braked. No skid!

"We'll make it now, everybody!" With my friends walking beside the Checker, I eased it back to Becky's house. They climbed in and we started out again. This time we made it.

At home, I marveled to my husband about God's answer.

"Ice doesn't have enough friction to keep the wheels from spinning," he explained. "You can stop or steer much easier on ice in neutral. Didn't I ever teach you that trick?"

No, he hadn't taught me that trick. But I won't forget the day God taught it to me!

Stick It Out Till June

RAY ORTLUND

hen Nels was in early high school, he wasn't applying himself and studying well. Having lunch one day with a friend, we were telling her how we were going bananas over our happy, unstructured, unmotivated, and unconcerned boy.

"I know what you mean!" said Marian. "Our Johnny was exactly the same. I don't think he ever would have turned out so well if we hadn't sent him to Stony Brook."

Stony Brook! We knew that fine Christian school outside New York City, and we asked Nels if he'd like to go. He was thrilled. Fifteen-year-old Nels dreamed of the glamour of an Eastern prep school and of wowing them with his personality and his tennis. . . .

It took him about a week to get thoroughly homesick. He decided that he was a true California beach boy and that from September to Christmas certainly ought to be as long as anyone should endure the East Coast.

Boy, did we have phone bills! He kept begging to come home at Christmas to stay, and we kept telling him he must complete that one school year.

"Nels," we said, "if you want to finish high school in California, we will love having you at home. But you really must stick out Stony Brook until June. You don't want to remember this as the year you were a quitter."

At Christmas he came home. He'd had a deep cold for three months, he was unbelievably skinny, and his face was all broken out. He looked terrible.

And he announced he'd sold his furniture, given up his dorm room, told everybody good-bye, and shipped home all his belongings.

"Well," we said, "we love you, Skipper, and when you're gone we miss you terribly, but you'll have to pay to ship your things back again. And you can just do without room furnishings until June."

He couldn't believe us! We said, "We don't want to spoil Christmas by arguing. Let's not talk about it until the Monday after Christmas, okay? Then we'll go spend the day in the desert and talk and pray together."

On December 29 the three of us drove to Palm Desert. By the end of the day Nels knew he'd lost, and it's a wrenching thing to see a skinny, six-foot-one lad cry. We sat there watching in agony as he paced back and forth in the sunshine he loved, and then he ended the discussion like this:

"All right, Mom and Dad, I'm going back. I hate it; I don't want to go, but you guys are forcing me."

(He wiped his runny nose with his hand, and when he heaved an uncontrollable sob, it just tore us apart.)

"But I just want you to know one thing. Even though I'm going back and I don't want to, we still love each other, and nothing is ever going to change that!"

Can't you believe how we were absolutely melted and how our hearts went out to him?

At that moment, and through the next six months, we prayed night and day for our dear boy. His cold continued to go in and out of pneumonia until spring, and he never did well scholastically. But can you imagine how continually and intensely we prayed over our dear, skinny, fragile, fifteen-year-old Nels? *He had surrendered himself in love to our will, and because of that he was in a distant and (to him) difficult place.*

"Lord," we prayed day and night, "ease his pain! Lord, give him godly friends! Lord, help him study! Lord, help him know we love him! Lord, help him see how those dear teachers and staff are on his side! Lord, dry up his cold! Lord, turn his thoughts to you! Lord, strengthen and help our dear boy! Lord, comfort him! Lord, help the time pass quickly until he's home!"

With April and May came thawing and more sunshine and more tennis, and Nels began to like it a little better. By June he was glad he'd stuck out the year, and by midsummer, at home, he had trouble deciding whether to go back and finish high school at Stony Brook.

He didn't—but he tells us that year was his most necessary and most life-changing year so far. We know it; we see it.

A little epilogue to the story came several years later when the three of us were dining in a local restaurant. Nels, rested, handsome, happy, and growing up, commented, "Mom and Dad, look across the room. There's_____who went back East to school the same fall I did and dropped out at Christmas time. Boy, I'm so glad I don't have to look back on that year and remember myself as a quitter."

Letting Go to Be Free

BECKY FREEMAN

rom my back porch one summer morning I watched an object lesson unfold, like some sweet story in a children's book.

The evening before, my children had found a baby blue jay struggling (and failing) to fly from the grass. To save the little foundling from becoming "dog food," they picked it up and brought the tiny creature to me. It opened its wide mouth expectantly. When it didn't get the desired worm right away, it began to chirp. Incessantly. So I mixed up some baby cereal with a little water and tried to feed the poor orphan. The results of our feeding time were similar to what happened when I tried to give my own babies their first spoonful of Pablum. More cereal landed on beak and feathers and the front of my shirt than went down the hungry throat of the baby bird. *There's more to being a mother bird than I bargained for,* I thought.

Finally, exhausted from effort, both the bird and I fell asleep. The next morning I awoke to a sharp series of chirps. "Look, little guy," I said loudly over his chirping, "I'd love to help you more than anything. But I just don't know how. Let's go look for your momma." I took my little noisemaker outside and balanced him carefully on the porch rail. Then I walked back inside the house and watched him from the sliding glass door. "Please, Lord," I prayed, "bring help!" I could hear the pitiful chirps through the glass.

Within a few seconds, the glorious sight of a mother bird flew into view. She coaxed the baby to follow her off the porch and up onto the safety of a nearby limb. "Yes!" I cheered from my observation point. "You can do it. Your mom's here now. Fly!" At that moment I spied a black-and-white cat slinking across the yard, looking exactly like Sylvester the cartoon cat. My heart stopped. My little "Tweety Bird" was a wobbly flyer at best. One false move and he would be breakfast.

Suddenly, a streak of blue plummeted from the sky and at-

tacked the stalking cat. Was it a plane? Was it Superman? No—
it was Daddy Bird to the rescue. I laughed in delight as I watched
the big blue jay tease and divert the attention of the cat, long
enough for Momma Bird to get Baby Bird to a higher perch. I
smiled, satisfied with the world, as I watched the family fly off
together and "Sylvester" still lickin' his frustrated chops.

Not audibly, but still plainly, I felt God saying to me, "This
was My lesson for you today, Becky. You are a 'fixer' by nature.
You enjoy the strokes you receive from helping others—from 'saving' them. But guess what? You can't fix everything that goes
wrong and everyone that is hurting. Sometimes, all you need to
do is *let* go. Stand and watch while I take care of the job. I have
plenty of momma and daddy birds in my kingdom who are often
more qualified to help than you are. Your 'job' in solving many
problems is to simply to let go, watch, and pray."

In how many areas could I apply this to my life—and possibly
find the peace I've been seeking?

Other Good Choices

KENDRA SMILEY

taught school for several years before my husband and I started our family. One year I had a group of fourth-graders who did not get along well. They argued and fussed with one another almost all the time. They were respectful to me and were good listeners, but they bickered endlessly with each other.

On one especially rough day, their arguing had pushed me to the edge. I'd had it with their bad attitudes. About three minutes before recess, I asked the class to take out paper and pencils.

"Please write your name at the top of your paper," I began. "On the next line I want you to write the name of the one person you would least like to sit by. Keep your papers covered."

"Do we only write one name?" many asked.

"Can I make a list?" asked one particularly disagreeable young man.

"Just one name," I replied and paused until the task was completed by everyone in class. "Now, number 1, 2, 3 on your paper and write three good things about the person you named. Write three things you could honestly praise about that person."

From the response of the students you would have thought I had just asked them to climb Mount Everest barefooted!

"I can't!"

"That's impossible!"

Knowing something about motivation and about fourth-graders, I replied, "And as soon as you are done, you may go outside for recess."

Needless to say, they all completed the assignment. Now, I would like to tell you that our little exercise revolutionized the classroom; that things were never the same again; that the students had respect and appreciation for one another for the rest of the year. I would like to tell you this, but I can't because I would be lying. They did, however, treat one another more kindly for a while. It did make a positive (if not eternal) difference in their attitudes and their interactions. Under my direction, those students chose to praise someone else and the arguing subsided. Choosing to praise another person is a good choice for a positive attitude.

Risky Grace

CHARLES R. SWINDOLL

 remember when I first earned my license to drive. I was about sixteen, as I recall. I'd been driving off and on for three years (scary thought, isn't it?). My father had been with me most of the time during my learning experiences, calmly sitting alongside me in the front seat, giving me tips, helping me know what to do. My mother usually wasn't in on those excursions because she spent more of her time biting her nails (and screaming) than she did advising. My father was a little more easygoing. Loud noises and screeching brakes didn't bother him nearly as much. My grandfather was the best of all. When I would drive his car, I would hit things . . . Boom! He'd say stuff like, "Just keep on going, Bud. I can buy more fenders but I can't buy more grandsons. You're learning." What a great old gentleman. After three years of all that nonsense, I finally earned my license.

I'll never forget the day I came in, flashed my newly acquired permit, and said, "Dad, look!" He goes, "Whoa! Look at this. You got your license. Good for you!" Holding the keys to his car, he tossed them in my direction and smiled, "Tell you what, son . . . you can have the car for two hours, all on your own." Only four words, but how wonderful: "All on your own."

I thanked him, danced out to the garage, opened the door, and shoved the key into the ignition. My pulse rate must have shot up to 180 as I backed out of the driveway and roared off. While cruising along "all on my own," I began to think wild stuff—like, *This car can probably do 100 miles an hour. I could go to Galveston and back twice in two hours if I averaged 100 miles an hour. I can fly down the Gulf Freeway and even run a few lights. After all, nobody's here to say "Don't!"* We're talking dangerous, crazy thoughts! But you know what? I didn't do any of them. I don't believe I drove above the speed limit. In fact, I distinctly remember turning in to the driveway early . . . didn't even stay away the full two hours. Amazing, huh? I had my dad's car all to myself with a full gas tank in a context of total privacy and freedom, but I didn't go crazy. Why? Relationship with my dad and my granddad was so strong that I couldn't, even though I had a license and nobody was in the car to restrain me. Over a period of time there had developed a sense of trust, a deep love relationship that held me in restraint.

After tossing me the keys, my dad didn't rush out and tape a sign on the dashboard of the car, "Don't you dare drive beyond the speed limit" or "Cops are all around the city, and they'll catch you, boy, so don't even think about taking a risk." He simply smiled and said, "Here are the keys, son, enjoy! What a demonstration of grace. And did I ever enjoy it! Looking back, now that I'm a father who has relived the same scene on four different occasions with my own children, I realize what a risk my father had taken.

Going Home

WILLIAM COLEMAN

ur first year of marriage ran like an old lawn mower. Some days it ran smoothly. Other days it wouldn't start. Sometimes our relationship sat motionless, going nowhere.

This happens to most lovers at some time, but we didn't know that then.

I was in graduate school. We were broke and far from family. Our efficiency apartment was one room and a bath. Life seemed overloaded with responsibility.

One evening, when life felt dull, I simply blurted out my frustration. "Pat," I began fearfully, "do you ever think about going home?"

Immediately she turned and gave me "that" look.

Every husband knows what "that" look means. Indeed everyone who had a mother knows "that" look.

Pat gave me her look and said without emotion, "Bill, I am home."

Stunned, I knew the discussion was over. She removed all uncertainty and eliminated any debate. Pat wasn't going anywhere. This left me with no choice but to work things out. Her response said our marriage was here to stay.

I thank God for a stubborn wife. If she had equivocated, argued or left a crack in the door I would have rushed in. Who knows what dumb thing I might have said? Our relationship could have been damaged beyond repair.

Sometimes love is at its best when it digs its heels in and holds tight.

Medicine for Monica

DEBORAH SILLAS NELL

he number twenty flashed above the gray lab door in the waiting room. I had two more numbers to go before it was my turn to have my blood drawn. My three-year-old daughter Sophie, who sat next to me, nudged my shoulder and said, "Mommy, why doesn't that girl lift up her head?" I turned to see whom she was talking about.

Sitting behind us was a man stroking his daughter's brown curly hair as her head lay on his lap.

"Well, I think she's sick, Sophie."

Her mother turned to us and smiled. "She's been throwing up for the last four days. She's very weak."

"Do the doctors know what's wrong?" I asked.

"No," replied the father. He turned to look at us. Dark circles surrounded his brown eyes. His face was unshaven.

"They are going to run some more tests to see what's wrong."

His hand stroked his daughter's curls.

"Do you want some water to drink?" asked the mother as she leaned toward her daughter.

The girl about the age of four slowly lifted her head. Damp hair stuck to her cheek. Her glazed eyes blinked, revealing long dark eyelashes. "Okay, Mommy."

Her mother held a red plastic cup to her mouth and her daughter slowly sipped some water.

Sophie, curious to get a closer look, had walked around to their seats and was intently looking at the girl and her family. I then noticed my number twenty-two flash over the lab door.

"Sophie, we need to go now. I have to get my blood drawn."

I took Sophie's hand and gently pulled her toward the lab door. Her body reluctantly followed, but her eyes never left the sick girl.

After my blood was drawn, we again saw the girl and her family in the waiting room. Sophie walked over to them and I followed. My heart, like Sophie's was drawn to this little girl and her family. An acquaintance of mine had just been through a bout of dehydration where she could keep nothing in her system. The doctors later found out that she had a parasite. I wondered if the doctors had ruled out parasites for this girl. As I mulled over these thoughts, the girl threw up the water she had just drunk. Her mother and father calmly wiped her mouth.

"Can I get you some paper towels?" I asked.

"Yes," her mother nodded.

Sophie and I walked to the restroom and brought back some wet and dry paper towels.

"Thank you." Her mother smiled as she took the towels from us.

Although it was a little awkward to keep standing there with them in the waiting room, I did not feel a peace about leaving. There was something more I needed to do.

I told the father about my friend's condition. "You might want to make sure they check for parasites," I added.

The father nodded.

I felt better about telling him but somehow I knew I needed to do more. Was I supposed to pray for the girl? Our pastor had been talking about following the prompting of the Holy Spirit and being obedient even when it was uncomfortable or seemed foolish. Just thinking about laying hands on this girl and praying for her in the waiting room increased my pulse rate dramatically. Deep in my spirit though, I knew that was what God was asking me to do. I took a deep breath and looked at the father.

"Would it be okay if I prayed for your daughter?"

The father looked at me with surprise but gently smiled. "That would be okay."

"What's your daughter's name?" I asked.

"Monica," he replied. "And your daughter? What's her name?"

"Sophie," I said. I put my hand on Sophie's shoulder and said, "Sophie, would you like to pray with me for Monica?"

"Okay," she said.

"Could we put our hands on Monica and pray for her?" I asked.

"Sure," said the father.

Sophie and I gently laid our hands on Monica's head.

Okay, God, help me to pray, I silently asked.

"Jesus, please help Monica to get better. Make the sickness go away," said Sophie sincerely, her eyes closed.

"Yes, Lord, heal Monica of this sickness. Give wisdom to the doctors to know what to do. Touch her body with your healing power that she may be well. We ask this in Jesus' name. Amen."

"Amen," repeated Sophie.

"Thank you," said the father.

"You're welcome," I said. "We will continue to pray for her."

As we walked out of the medical building, I was still a little shaken. *Did we just pray for a stranger in a waiting room? Did our prayers make any difference?*

I never expected to see Monica and her family again but about six months later we ran into them at the grocery store. I would not have recognized them had the father not approached us. He and Monica walked up to us as we were waiting in the check-out line.

"Do you remember us?" he asked Sophie and bent down to look into her eyes. "You prayed for Monica when she was really sick."

I looked at the father and then at the girl with the big bright eyes. They looked somewhat familiar but I could not place them. And then it all came back to me.

"She got better!" I said.

"Yes. It was going to take two weeks to get the results of that test they took. So I took her to my doctor. He said she had an infection in her stomach. He gave her some medicine and she got better. But she got better because you prayed for her."

Monica smiled at us shyly.

"Thank you," said the father. He and Monica walked over to his wife who was waiting in the next line.

His words echoed in my mind. "She got better because you prayed for her."

I knew it was God that made her better and not our prayers. Yet God had used Sophie and me to reach out to a sick girl and make a difference.

"Thank You, Lord," I silently prayed. "Thank You for healing Monica and thank You for letting us know that You did heal her. You are an awesome God!"

Surprising Answers

TERRY FITZGERALD SIECK

oke! Coke! Coke!" My three-year-old grandson, Bijan, yelled as he rounded the corner to our kitchen. We'd been working on manners, so I dutifully replied, "You may have a Coca-Cola, but what do you say first?"

"Pease." Although he had trouble saying "L's," Bijan had no problem making his wishes known. I poured the amber liquid into his cup. "Now what do you say?"

He raised the mug, grinned, and chimed, "Cheers!" I laughed. It was not the "thank you" that I had been expecting, but was certainly a great answer.

Months later as I recalled this incident, I thought about how I had come to be Bijan's grandmother. My husband, Ron, and I had been married 15 years. We were both professional people, only children with no children of our own. As we were departing on a long awaited vacation, Ron became ill. He died two weeks later. At age forty-four, I was devastated and alone. My parents had died. My remaining "close" family, two aunts and a stepmother, lived far away. Fortunately, I had a lot of friends. And, I had God.

God and I got to know each other a lot better in the ensuing months. Not that He didn't know me, but I needed to get to know Him. I prayed and prayed. I sent Him list after list of what I wanted and thought I needed in my life. At the top of one list was an exciting job, at the top of another, a nice new husband.

Nothing seemed to happen until one day when a Christian friend suggested I tear up my lists and send God a blank piece of paper. I dropped to my knees and prayed anew, "I've been sending you my lists all these months. I was wrong. Send me your list for my life. But make it clear. Bang me over the head with it. You know I'm a stubborn Swede!"

When I finally relinquished my will to God, His list—His answers to my prayers—started to come. I went back to school for a Master's Degree, something that wasn't on my list, and then found an exciting job. However, no new husband materialized.

Ever the list maker, I had someone specific in mind. He was tall, dark, handsome, the prince charming of all the fairy tales. Alas, I was no Cinderella and he fell in love with someone else. I was devastated again. And, again, I had to relinquish my will to the Master's.

I prayed. I waited. I prayed more. I waited impatiently. I tried finding someone myself. I made a mess of things. I prayed. I waited. I looked, but didn't see anyone.

Fortunately, there was someone who saw me: a good Christian man, whose dark hair had turned silver, not too tall, but not too short, and certainly handsome. Larry Sieck was on the board of directors of the charity where I worked. I had heard he was widowed, but had dismissed him as too old. My husband had been fifty when he died, I thought a younger man was a safer bet.

Then, one evening after a meeting, I introduced myself to Larry and mentioned that I, too, had been widowed. Surprised, he confided that he had been widowed twice. Then he suggested we get together for a cup of coffee . . . sometime. I, off-handedly, replied, "Oh, sure."

The next morning at 9:05 he called. We had lunch. I discovered that his gray hair came from experience, not age. Lunch led to dinner, dinner led to romance, and a year and a half later, Larry and I were married.

Larry didn't come into our marriage all by himself. He brought with him lots of family: three married daughters, a brother, sister, aunts, uncles, nieces, nephews, and a grandson, Bijan. Other grandchildren soon followed: Olivia, Cameron, and Harrison. They are the lights of my life.

When I think of Bijan, I often remember that day in the kitchen, handing him a Coke and expecting him to say "Thank you." "Cheers!" was a much better answer. When I think about looking for a husband, I recall my prayers for the tall, dark, handsome prince charming. Larry Sieck was a much better answer. Like Bijan's reply, God's was a happy surprise. I not only got a wonderful husband, but a whole new family: just what I needed, more than I asked for, and beyond what I envisioned. Although I'm still tempted to send God a list from time to time, I've learned an important lesson: God's provision is far more abundant than my imagination. Trust Him.

Sand Dollars and Stinky Fish

DEBRA WEST SMITH

 loved walking the beach at dawn. It's like a treasure hunt following the wavy line of debris left by the evening tide. With the same anticipation that I felt searching through a bundle of mail or a stuffed gift bag, I grabbed a cup of coffee and went out early. The sky was baby-pink and the sun still a promise. The wet sand was cold between my toes and tiny footprints like some exotic Eastern script told me that I was not the "earliest bird" after all.

Nestled in the wet sand were many broken shells. The fragments varied in size, color, and shape, each a testimony to our Creator's imagination. I wandered, hoping to find an undamaged specimen. I hardly noticed the stinky fishhead until I almost stepped on it.

"Gross!" I said to the laughing gulls. Wrinkling my nose, I stepped around the remains of the fish. But, almost against my will, I kept looking back. The lifeless eyes bulged and the mouth gaped open. The meat had been torn away from the spine by one of the dangers fish face.

Though I walked on, the smell stayed with me. I chose each step carefully. Where there was one dead fish, there could be more. Instead of searching the waves for treasure, I was now more concerned with not stepping on something unpleasant. I wandered down the beach, suspiciously watching each wave that lapped near my feet. Sure enough, there was another one.

A voice surprised me from behind. It was one of my children, holding some exciting find. I waited, wondering what it could be. After all, I had just come that way and didn't find any good shells.

"Look!" she cried. "A sand dollar. I've never found a whole one before."

I studied the fragile white disc that is said to represent Christ. On the front was traced a lily shape, a tiny star as its center. This was surrounded by five holes—four nail holes and a fifth made by a Roman spear. The back was etched with a poinsettia that reminds us of Christmas. I'd never found a whole sand dollar either—just broken pieces.

"How did I miss it?" I wondered. "I just came that way and all I found were stinky fish."

But even as I spoke, I knew the answer—what we seek is often what we find.

Sweet As Strawberries

CAROL RUSSELL

hat are they doing?" I asked as we drove up the lane of my in-laws' farm. Dad drove the tractor slowly through the garden, pulling a large wooden farm wagon, and Mom shoveled something out of it.

"They are putting chicken manure on the strawberries," Bob said.

"How disgusting!" I declared. Bob laughed at me as he got out of the car.

Bob and I waved at them, then sat on the back porch steps while they finished their task. Laurie Ann, our two-year-old, began playing with the cats that had wandered up from the barn.

I watched Bob's folks as they worked and thought about how little I knew about farming and growing things. I was a city girl. Every time we came to the farm, I learned something new.

"Hi, you two," Dad said as he came across the yard. "Bob, I'm glad you're here. I need you to look at that tractor. I think I have a problem."

As Dad and Bob walked off, Mom bent down and stole a kiss from her granddaughter. Pulling off her gloves and sitting next to me on the steps, she sighed, "That's hard on old backs."

"I don't see how you do it," I said. "I just can't imagine standing in that wagon, shoveling that stuff."

"Well, it isn't my favorite job and it certainly isn't the nicest, but all jobs can't be nice and smell good. It's important, you know. If we want good sturdy plants and have them produce good fruit, then we have to care for them. It starts with planting. Then begins the weeding and watering. They have to be nourished. That includes putting fertilizer on them. It will make the largest and sweetest berries."

"Thanks, but I think I'll just use sugar on my strawberries."

Mom laughed and said, "It's work, but the fruit we have in the end is worth it. You two go on in the house. I have to put away a few things and then I'll be in."

Later, as Mom was placing glasses of milk on the table, her next question, "Well, how are things going?" sent me into a long discourse of my trials and tribulations.

"That old wringer washer is broke again. We need an automatic, but the money just isn't there. I'm not sure it will last through another baby."

Mom sliced two large pieces of bread from her homemade loaf.

"I guess Bob will just have to fix it again," I said.

She began to toast the bread.

"The cost of Laurie's medicine went up again. Every time I have that prescription refilled, the cost goes up."

She set the plate of toast on the table and walked to the refrigerator. I lifted Laurie, putting her into the high chair and continued my complaining.

"They changed Bob's hours at work. He is still early morning man at the station, but now he has two hours in the morning when he comes home and then has to go back. It sure has messed up our schedule."

Mom took out a bowl of strawberry preserves and placed it on the table. We said grace and then began to enjoy our snack.

"I know what the Bible says," I continued, "and I know what Matthew 6 says. God tells us that He watches the sparrows and cares for the lilies of the field. I know He loves and cares for us and that we shouldn't worry about tomorrow and about 'things.' It's hard, Mom. The harder we try, the harder it gets."

Thoughtfully Mom placed a spoonful of preserves on the corner of her toast.

"Perhaps," she said, "God is just putting fertilizer on His strawberries."

I never looked at strawberries—or trials—the same again.

"Turkey Red"

ESTHER LOEWEN VOGT

s a writer, I often receive notes from editors offering me writing jobs. In the spring of 1974 when David C. Cook invited me to enter their juvenile book contest, I shrugged it off. As much as I loved to write, I didn't see how I could squeeze in the time. Our youngest daughter was to be married on May 30, and our old house needed to be perked up for company. Working as a nurse's aide at the local nursing home, I knew time was of the essence. Besides, we'd planned to visit our older daughter over the Easter weekend. How could I possibly paint and paper, clean the house from top to bottom, take a trip—and still work on a book?

No way, I decided. *If the Lord wants me to tackle a writing project, He'll have to create a special time for it.*

On Palm Sunday, my husband and I took our son to catch a bus in a nearby town. We were almost home when we slammed into a tree. My husband Curt suffered only a few facial scratches. But pain jabbed my left ankle and left arm and I suspected fractures. The hospital x-rays verified the break in my left wrist and a compound fracture in my left ankle. During my nineteen-day hospital stay, I realized I'd be laid up for some time and we wouldn't be able to go on our trip. After I was stabilized, I began to hear a phrase running through my mind over and over, like a broken record: "Now you'll have time to write that book . . . Now you'll have time to write that book . . . Now you'll have time . . ."

One night the nurse refused to give me a sleeping pill. I tossed and turned for what seemed like hours until my watch dial said 2:30.

"Okay, Lord," I said finally, "obviously You want me to enter the contest, so would You *please* tell me what the plot is going to be for that children's book?" I wasn't enthusiastic at all about the whole idea.

As Mennonites, we had just celebrated the centennial of the

Mennonite migration from Europe to America. I remembered stories my Grandma Loewen had told me when she came to America from the Ukraine in the 1870's. Right then, I pulled together an outline for a story about ten-year-old Martha Friesen and her journey from Russia to Kansas. I titled it *Turkey Red* because of the turkey-red hard winter wheat Mennonites had brought to America in the 1870's. My plot fell into place and I rolled over and went to sleep.

Several weeks later, I hobbled down the church aisle on crutches as the "mother of the bride" at our daughter's wedding. After we'd swept up the rice, I settled down to write my story by longhand with my injury-free hand. By deadline time, the cast was off my arm and I typed up *Turkey Red* and sent it to the contest.

Awards would be made around Christmastime but by Christmas I hadn't heard anything. Even January passed uneventfully. Obviously *Turkey Red* hadn't made it. I brashly wrote the editor and asked him to return my manuscript.

Then one day in early February a phone call came from editor Dean Merrill. He explained, "We received two excellent entries but we couldn't decide which of the two should win the prize. We finally decided to award two prizes. *Turkey Red* will receive second place with a $150 cash award and $1,500 advance on future publication. Is that agreeable?"

I sat down slowly and drew a very shaky breath. All I could think of was Romans 8:28: "For all things work together for good to them that love God and are called according to His purpose." I saw how God had worked out everything to give me time to write my story! In the accident my head wasn't hurt and I could think; I wasn't really sick, just laid up. Also it was my *right arm*—my writing arm—that was spared. My left arm was healed by the time I needed to type up the final draft. God had arranged everything to give me time to write that juvenile story! He knew all the time I would be a winner but He had to make me willing to write it. God's grace and leading had been abundantly evident even though I hadn't initially seen it.

That children's book, *Turkey Red,* and two sequels, have sold well for over 20 years. When I think back and realize the number of children who might have missed that story if I hadn't written it, I almost shiver. Since then when God tells me to "write," I don't hesitate. I write!

Setting My Heart

JANE C. KONING

hen is your next bicycle trip?" Kathleen asked me as we were driving home with our husbands after seeing a play in San Diego. Enthusiastically, I told her about the trip I planned to take for four days with my bicycling friend, Pat. In fact, the prospect of that trip had kept me going while I cared for my three-year-old twin grandchildren for several days while their mother recovered from childbirth.

The day of our departure, we first met with our Bible Study Group to discuss our lesson on "The Inner Life" from J. Heinrich Arnold's book, *Discipleship: Living for Christ in the Daily Grind.* The last question stated: "An attachment is anything other than God that drives you or defines who you are. It is something you would find terribly difficult to live without even though you don't really need it. Do you have any attachments? Ask God to show you where you may be overly attached." I didn't have to ask God because I already knew. Aside from being with my family, bicycling and hiking were what I loved to do most. Those activities defined who I was.

My friends and family saw me as a person who loved to plan and go on short- and long-distance rides and hikes. I even rationalized it by thinking of it as a kind of ministry for my working friends who didn't have the time to plan these activities but needed them to ease the stress in their lives. But basically, my motives were self-centered—I needed someone to go with!

My focus needed to change from seeking temporary happiness from my next bicycle trip to having the lasting joy that comes from putting God first in my life. I asked Him to help me by changing my desires. He answered in an unusual way.

During the four-day trip, our route and plans had to be changed, which annoyed and disappointed me. Several days later, I went with two friends for a day's ride on the Angeles Crest Highway. The beginning of the route involved a five-mile uphill climb and then a five-mile descent. When we arrived at the crest, my two friends seemed reluctant to ride the five miles down because they would have to ride up again on the return trip. Again, I was annoyed. We were in a beautiful mountain setting and had seen several beautiful waterfalls, which were unusual for July. How could they, in all this beauty, not want to continue to see what lay ahead? How could they be content to reach a certain level and then stop, not wanting to undertake a challenging but also rewarding return? I tried to mask my irritation with encouraging words like "You can do it. I know the road levels out after a while."

They overcame their reluctance and we continued to our destination. On the return uphill ride, I was still feeling annoyed with them. I had taken them to unusual places they never would have gone on their own. Couldn't they trust me in this situation? Did they only want to go on the easy, familiar rides?

As these thoughts were churning around in my mind, God reminded me that I am like that in my Christian life. He wants to bring me to a higher level of faith and service, but I am reluctant, afraid of the commitment and sacrifice; not trusting God's strength to help me and not realizing the rewards which follow.

On my refrigerator I have a picture of two bicyclists on top of a hill with some clouds in the background and the words, "Since you have been raised with Christ, set your heart on the things above, not on earthly things." What seemed to me to be annoying events were really God's answer to my prayer. Instead of seeking my joy and purpose in outdoor activity, my joy will come from obedience to His command to abide in His love, and love others as He has loved me.

The Appointment

BEVERLY HAMEL

n unsaved acquaintance and I drove from Kansas City back home to San Diego several years ago. It was a great way to get home cheaply to see the family as well as drop off Christmas presents. But it had been difficult going with her because she didn't want me to talk about Jesus at all. But the Lord planned a meeting with her, anyway.

Mary and I had seen lots of snow on that thirty-six-hour rush that October day. We usually drove straight through except to exchange drivers and eat. We never stopped at any hotels to sleep, but instead, slept in the back seat when our driving shift was over. But that one cold early morning, we were both fatigued at the same time so we parked at a rest stop in the mountains over Flagstaff, Arizona, to sleep for a couple of hours. We agreed to leave again at six in the morning.

I always sleep like a log and rarely wake up at night, but my eyes shot wide open around 5:15 A.M., thinking I heard a voice. When I saw the time, I was about to go back to sleep, when I heard it again. It was just as urgent as I remembered. "Beverly! Wake up! Get out of here!"

I knew Mary wasn't going to like me waking her up on the basis of my intuition, but I did anyway. She wasn't a happy camper! Though she was miffed at me, she drove the car out of the rest area immediately.

As we left the mountains and descended to the desert floor, we listened to the radio and heard that the mountains were being bombarded with a snowstorm and people were being stranded. I looked at Mary and we both realized it was the very same level of the mountain that we had been sleeping on just an hour before.

At first, I was shocked; then I began to silently give God a clap offering. But I also knew God does things to bring glory to Himself. When we were on the mountain and I was trying to urge Mary to leave right away, I didn't tell her about the Lord's voice.

I did then. "I've had the Lord come to my aid before. Although I very rarely hear audible warnings, I just know that whenever I ignore them, I have very difficult times."

But Mary couldn't understand. She didn't show any amazement, but shifted in her seat and kept on driving. It was another seed dropped into her heart whether she wanted it or not. Shifting in her seat was a dead give-away. And I believe she'll never forget that day; I never have.

$\mathcal{W}$e all need hope desperately. Without it, we are like balloons with a slow leak. Yet when we concentrate on God's abundant ability to love us and come to our rescue, the leak is healed and our spirits are buoyant again. Let's share that hope with everyone.

We have this hope as an anchor for the soul,
firm and secure.

HEBREWS 6:19 (NIV)

The Abundant Problem Solver

CHARLOTTE H. BURKHOLDER

he mountains beyond my picture window shimmered with beauty in the morning sun, but my blank stare registered nothing. The ache in my heart bounced around like a hard rubber ball until my heart became a throbbing mass of pain. Watching a loved one go through divorce and feeling powerless to help is an immobilizing kind of pain.

I numbly forced myself to follow through with the day's plans, which included going to a spring daffodil show. As I entered the door, the scent of thousands of blooming daffodils greeted me. Nodding their brilliant heads, they seemed to be hiding some happy secret from me. Taking a seat as far back in the corner as I could, I tried to concentrate on the speaker's comments, hoping the fake smile on my face didn't look as fake as it felt.

"We have 400 different varieties of daffodils," the speaker continued.

That single thought stuck with me as I drove home. Four hundred different varieties of daffodils! *Why would God create 400 varieties of daffodils when He knows the smallness of my human mind can't possibly comprehend a fraction of that? And that's just daffodils!* I mused. *Think of all the hundreds—no, thousands of other flowers! And that's just flowers!*

Think of all the rest of His creation . . . the grasses, trees, insects, animals, sea creatures! Why does God go to such extravagance when I am incapable of taking it all in or being able to appreciate it fully?

As my heart rose in worship to such a marvelous Creator, He quietly gave me the answer.

"It's to show you," He whispered in my heart, "that I have abundant ways of solving your problems. As you cannot comprehend the extent of my created world, so you have no idea of the countless resources I have for helping you."

The throbbing ache gave way to joyous wonder. And now I know the secret within their nodding yellow heads.

Flickers of Hope

BARBARA JOHNSON

 recall speaking at a weekend conference and then catching a plane for home. We came in over Los Angeles at night, and from my window seat I saw thousands of flickering lights below. The pilot's voice crackled over the intercom informing us he was making his final approach, but I really didn't hear much of what he was saying. I was thinking about ALL those lights, realizing that each one represented a home where there was (or probably would be) pain of some kind, because pain is inevitable in this life.

My imagination started working overtime, and I began seeing each light as a painful abscess that needed to be drained—but how? I have always loved the bit of wisdom that says:

> Even if it burns a bit low at times,
> the secret of life is to always
> keep the flame of hope alive.

Gazing below, I began to fear my "flame" had flickered out someplace along the way because it all seemed so overwhelmingly HOPELESS. Then it struck me that I knew better. Hope was supposed to be my specialty, and here I was seemingly drained of all hope myself! I realized that speaking at all those conferences had sapped my spirit. I was suffering a mild case of burnout. My batteries needed recharging, and what better place to go for that than the promises of Scripture?

> I will . . . transform her valley of troubles
> into a door of hope. (Hos. 2:15 TLB)

> There is hope for your future,
> says the lord, and your children
> will come again to their own
> land. (Jer. 31:17 TLB)

In the next few moments my vision from the airline window cleared. The scene below DID NOT represent hopeless pain. Instead, each flickering light in that giant sprawl known as the L.A. Basin was really a place where God's redeeming love could bring hope if only those in pain were willing to LET HIM IN. Then the abscesses could be lanced, and healing could begin.

Ultimate Bereavement

H. NORMAN WRIGHT

ur son Matthew died at the age of twenty-two. He was a profoundly mentally retarded child and at his death was about eighteen months old mentally. He lived in our home until he was eleven and then lived at Salem Christian Home in Ontario, California. At the age of twenty-one he developed a condition known as reflux esophagitis, a burning of the lining of the esophagus. He was given medication, but after that didn't work, Matthew went into the hospital for corrective surgery. Following the surgery, complications and infection set in. After a week had passed, additional surgery was performed.

My wife Joyce tells what happened next in her own words:

"As I visited each day, our time together was special. I patted Matthew's hand and talked to him in simple, loving words. He didn't reach out and respond, but his eyes followed me as I moved about the room. It was touching to see him content and peaceful, even during his times of discomfort.

"I was aware of God's presence through the days at the hospital. I was reassured that He was in control, and I had a sense of being uplifted by the prayers of family and friends. I was even able to reach out to a family dealing with their son's tragic motorcycle accident, which had caused massive trauma to his head.

"After a week, additional surgery was performed. Following the operation, Matthew stayed in the intensive care unit. He was heavily sedated and unconscious. There were eight tubes in him, and he was constantly on a ventilator. He developed adult respiratory disorder syndrome. We were hopeful when the fever dropped and his blood pressure stabilized, but in several days we could see that he was not responding. The doctors felt he was in the Lord's hands. We prayed at his bedside for the Lord's will to be done.

"We had stayed at our home the night of March 14 instead of at a motel near the Loma Linda Hospital. I woke up at 4:00 A.M.

with the feeling that Matthew was worse. I called the hospital, and the staff confirmed my fears. They had gone to full power on the ventilator. Around 7:00 that morning, as we were getting ready for the day, we received a phone call. It was one of the medical staff, and he said, "We would like you to come to the hospital as soon as possible." His request didn't need any amplification.

"Fortunately, we were able to speed through the traffic those sixty miles to the hospital. Both of us were aware that it could be Matthew's final hour. We had not seen any response from him for days.

"Norm and I walked into the room, and the doctors told us that Matthew's lungs and heart were failing and would probably stop in about an hour. My initial response, which might surprise you if you've never had a loved one suffer and die, was profound joy. I was truly happy for him. I said, 'Oh, he'll be in the presence of the Lord this day!' I knew he would be finished with the struggles of this world, totally healed and finally out of pain.

"We both felt that way. But we also felt helpless since there was nothing anyone could do to make Matthew well again. As much as we knew he was going to a far better place, we also knew we were facing the greatest loss of our lives.

"We said good-bye to Matthew, and I prayed at his bedside, thanking the Lord for our precious child and for His provision of eternal life. As we stood there, we saw Matthew's pulse rate decline ten beats. We felt as though we were giving him back to God and saying, 'He's Yours. Have Your perfect will with him.' We believed God had something better for him.

"Matthew's decreasing vital signs confirmed the reality that he was going to die soon. The doctors said we could stay there or wait in a family room, and we chose the latter. Within an hour, the doctors came to tell us Matthew had died. We cried and talked with them. God was truly loving and merciful when He took Matthew home that day, and we bowed to His perfect will. Perhaps others won't understand our mixture of feelings, but that's all right. We felt at peace.

"Losing Matthew was a tremendous blow in and of itself. But like any major loss, it also caused a number of additional, or secondary, losses. The routine we had followed for years was gone forever. We would no longer look through catalogs to select his special sleepwear. We wouldn't have the special weekends in which he would come home and stay overnight, nor would we be able to stop by Salem House to take him out to eat. Instead, we would drive past where he used to live and keep traveling along the freeway."

Even now, several years after the death of our son, Joyce and I still experience a sense of dullness or feeling down on what would have been Matthew's birthday. And when March 15 rolls around each year, we're especially sensitive, because that's when he died.

There is no easy way to recover. Losing a child is truly the ultimate bereavement.

God allows suffering so that we can enter into another person's sorrow and affliction. Joyce and I have experience this numerous times as couples have sought us out either because they have a disabled child or have lost a child in death. Because we have already walked the path they are now walking, they want to talk with us.

When you experience a crisis in your life, you will have compassion and understanding for others going through the same experience. Suffering gives us the opportunity to learn to give thanks in very situation and event of life.

"Adios, Ross"

BOB BUFORD

y son Ross—our only son—was a person of great promise. He was my heir, my successor, and, in many ways that may seem odd to you but absolutely real to me, one of my greatest heroes.

After Ross graduated from Texas Christian University in Fort Worth, he moved to Denver to take a job as an investment banker. It was preparation for the time when he would come back to Texas to join the family business and eventually take a leadership position in it. He made $150,000 his first full year of work in the deal-making business, and his second year—only barely begun— would likely have sent his income soaring to over $500,000. There was big money to be made in his line of work in the late 1980's. But far more important than his financial successes, Ross was a good human being—determined, energetic, caring—with wonderful people skills. He had many friends, and he loved life in all its pleasures and ambiguities.

On the evening of January 3, 1987, I received a call from my brother Jeff, who told me that Ross and two of his friends had attempted to swim the Rio Grande River, which separates South Texas from Mexico.

"I think we have serious trouble," Jeff told me in a voice that meant it. "Ross is missing in the Rio Grande."

It was a lark that led the three young men to the Rio Grande: They wanted to experience what it was like for illegal aliens to cross the watery border into a land of promise. Ross was twenty-four years old, and it was the last adventure of his life on earth.

My brother informed me that the Texas Rangers were coordinating the search for Ross and one of his companions; the third young man was alive and frantic about the fate of his friends. I flew down to the Rio Grande Valley to join in the search, arriving by daybreak the next morning. I hired airplanes, helicopters, boats, trackers with dogs—everything that money could buy.

By three o'clock in the afternoon, I looked into the eyes of one of the trackers and knew that I would never see Ross again in this life.

I remember walking along a limestone bluff perhaps two hundred feet above the muddy and treacherous river, as frightened as I've ever felt. *Here's something you can't dream your way out* of, I told myself. *Here's something you can't think your way out of, buy your way out of, or work your way out of.*

It was all too clear in this maddening solitude on the river bluff. *This is,* I thought to myself, *something you can only trust your way out of.*

The incomprehensible was breaking out all around me, and there was no way I could understand it apart from an eternal perspective. Albert Einstein once said that "what is incomprehensible is beyond the realm of science. It is in the realm of God." This was truly in the realm of God.

I remember sending up a prayer that in retrospect seems to be the most intelligent petition I ever made to heaven. "Dear God," I pleaded, "somehow give me the ability to accept and absorb whatever grace people might bring to me at this terrible time. Amen."

The search for Ross and his friend continued, and grace abounded in my life and relationships. They found Ross' body in the spring, more than four months later, about ten miles downriver. Before his body was recovered, we had found on his desk at home in Denver a handwritten copy of his will, dated February 20, 1986, less than a year before the river swallowed his body. Through that long winter of fear and uncertainty, his words were also a grace to me.

"Well, if you're reading my will, then, obviously, I'm dead," Ross began. "I wonder how I died? Probably suddenly, because otherwise I would have taken the time to rewrite this. Even if I am dead, I think one thing should be remembered, and that is that I had a great time along the way. More importantly, it should be noted that I am in a better place now."

The will directed how he wanted his earthly goods distributed, and Ross concluded the document with this benediction: "In closing, I loved you all and thank you. You've made it a great life. Make sure you all go up instead of down and I'll be waiting for you at heaven's gate. Just look for the guy in the old khakis, Stetson, and faded shirt, wearing a pair of Ray-Bans and a Jack Nicholson smile. I also thank God for giving me the chance to write this before I departed. Thanks. Adios, Ross."

As horrifying and sad as it was, and is, to have lost him, Ross' disappearance and death also provided the greatest moments of rare insight and grandest gestures of immeasurable grace and joy that I ever hope to experience. Utter emptiness and brokenness left me feeling awful and wonderful at the same time. Close and silent embraces from friends, letters and phone calls of concern and empathy, and gifts of meals prepared and brought to our home were much-needed signs of love. One letter, in particular, showed us just how much Ross' life had been a witness to those around him:

> Dear Mr. and Mrs. Buford,
>
> Ross and I were best friends. All that he had, Ross shared with me. He shared his thoughts and ideas, his pleasures and his pains; he shared a whole lot of laughter. But most of all, he shared his love.
>
> Well, now Ross has a new best friend. And now Ross is with his new best friend. But just as before, Ross continues to share. Today, Ross is sharing his new best friend with his old best friend. I thank the Lord God for Ross, and I thank Ross for the Lord God.
>
> Ronnie

Despite the comfort of those words, I was forced to lean on God entirely in those dark weeks after Ross' death, to think often of the Scripture verse "Trust in the Lord with all your heart, and lean not to your own understanding." I learned that God truly is sufficient and that His strength is made perfect in weakness.

Bearing Children

JO FRANZ

he hysterectomy dashed to pieces my hope of ever bearing a child. Sorrow bore down on my heart, like the weight of a heavy shield placed over my chest during dental x-rays. I told myself it must be for the best since I was already in my mid-thirties and I suffered from multiple sclerosis. Yet the finality of my lost dream left an aching hole. I exhorted myself, *You don't have time to indulge in self-pity, there's work to be done!*

With sun pouring in the patio window, I vocalized higher and higher. My solo concert scheduled for Galilee Baptist Church was only three weeks away. My vocal chords and diaphragm needed shaping up after major surgery. Besides, singing praise to God in painful circumstances had become strong, sweet medicine for whatever ailed me over the years. My focus invariably transferred from myself to my Lord whose love and knowledge of all things comforted me.

Suddenly, an out-of-tune ring pierced my song. Hanging onto furniture and walls because of coordination and balance difficulties, I made my way to the phone.

"Hi," the stranger began. "I saw your advertisement in Galilee Church. I was wondering, were you treated by a physical therapist named Sherri twelve years ago?"

Amazed, I exclaimed, "Yes, I was."

"That woman was me! I'm so glad to be able to thank you after all these years for sharing Christ with me. I've continued to grow as a Christian and I just wanted you to know!"

As Sherri spoke about her changed life and involvement in church, I remembered Paul calling Timothy his "true son in the faith" (1 Timothy 1:2). I had taken part in a special birth, after all, and songs of praise to God heralded His reminder. In fact, as I recalled the many times I had shared Jesus' good news with others, I realized I had taken part in "bearing" many children—spiritually. Memories of so many flooded my mind and the aching hole filled with joy.

The Lord abundantly provided grace to deal with my loss through Sherri's call, just as He had abundantly provided opportunities to work along with the Holy Spirit in "bearing" children for God.

The Sparrow and I

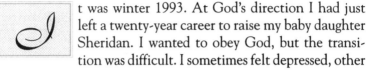t was winter 1993. At God's direction I had just left a twenty-year career to raise my baby daughter Sheridan. I wanted to obey God, but the transition was difficult. I sometimes felt depressed, other times doubted the decision I'd made, and frequently sensed loneliness wrapping its gray mantle around my heart. Sometimes God seemed absent, as if hibernating. I often felt empty—a powerful parallel to winter's stark lifelessness.

In my study one snowy afternoon, I noticed a child playing with her father in the neighboring yard. Garbed in a bright red coat, she was a crimson cardinal punctuating whiteness—the only splash of color I'd seen in days. She'd flutter through snow, fall, then be swept into her father's loving embrace—only to flutter, then fall again. Her father stood ever present to scoop her to his breast.

And what of the Heavenly Father? Although Scripture doesn't refer to cardinals, I knew Jesus said that not one lowly sparrow can fall apart from God's knowledge. Not one! I knew I was of more value than *many* sparrows.

The truth was plain. Would my Father God do less for me than He did for sparrows or than my neighbor did for his child? Had I fallen without His notice? Would He not take my hand as I reached for His?

Hedged in doubt and resistance, I hadn't reached out. That afternoon, as I *finally* cried out to God in my prayer journal, He made me profoundly aware of His abundant care and presence. I penned the following poem after that time of prayer. And in the six years since I wrote it, God has abundantly met all my needs.

MIDWINTER PROMISE

"Are not two sparrows sold for a cent?
And yet not one of them
will fall to the ground

apart from your Father.
But the very hairs of your head
are all numbered.
Therefore do not fear;
you are of more value
than many sparrows." —Matthew 10:29–31

Winter lingers.
Skies lie still,
white as whalebones,
scrimshawed with bare branches.

God hibernates
while unheard prayers reverberate
like echoes in hollow caves.
Snowbound earth sleeps
silently,
cold as bone-filled graves.

Night tarries, until a child arrayed in red,
bright as any cardinal,
hops through snow, then falls.
Her father stoops
to lift her wounded pride.

How can my Father, sleeping, know
the flight and fall of cardinals—lowly sparrows?

God never slumbers, never sleeps.
He lifts my head,
then strokes and numbers every hair
like strands of sand,
innumerable along a shore.

It's I, of fledgling faith, who sleeps,
who's hedged in doubt's midwinter.
I can but lift my wounded pride—
implore the grace of One Who cares,
Who does not sleep nor hide.

"A Very Present Help in Trouble"

MARGARITA GARZA DE BECK

hanks for letting us know, Sally," I said. "Tell Dean and Shari we'll keep them in our prayers." My hand lingered on the receiver long after I'd hung up the phone. It was my husband's sister calling to tell us her daughter-in-law Shari had just delivered twin girls. But they were premature and too tiny to survive. My thoughts traveled back nearly thirty-five years to a similar experience in my own life when my premature twins died.

I'd felt miserable all six months of my pregnancy. The doctor could tell that I was getting very large very fast and he often reprimanded me for gaining too much weight. Then, one day as I was about to leave his office, he suddenly decided to check my blood pressure again. For the first time, he looked concerned.

My blood pressure was too high. He ordered me to bed, but it was too late for precautions. Less than 24 hours later I went into labor.

At the hospital, after fourteen hours of labor at home, a nurse listened to my abdomen. Finally she said, "You're going to have twins!" Twins? I could hardly believe it. I was so miserable by that time, though, that I couldn't concentrate on what that would mean for us.

There was a lot of confusion in my room with nurses coming in and out. My mother caught part of one conversation. "She has toxemia." That didn't tell Mom anything. All she knew was that for the next ten hours I was delirious and getting worse as the hours went by.

Saturday morning the doctor's voice broke through to me. I had delivered two tiny boys. The doctor came to talk to me again when I was back in my room. He said something about the smaller twin having difficulty breathing. Both twins had been put into incubators.

"No need for concern," I told myself as I drifted back to sleep. "The incubators will help them . . . no problem . . ."

I slept most of the day. By suppertime I was awake and anxious to see our sons. I walked to the nursery and beheld our firstborn sons. My arms ached to hold them, even to touch them, but their glass cages allowed me only to look at them.

"They're so darling," I exclaimed to the nurse, "identical, and so dark!" The nurse avoided my eyes as she scurried me back to my room.

Jim waved as he passed my room. "I'm going down to see the babies. Be right back, Hon."

I waited . . . and waited. My parents waited with me. When Jim came back, we were all puzzled. He came into my room sobbing, unable to utter a word.

A nurse came in at that moment. Little Jeff had just died. Little Jimmy was experiencing the same problems. We weren't to get our hopes up too high for him, either.

I looked at Mom through my tears. My eyes glared, "Where is God now?" Two hours later the nurse came in again. This time there was only numbness and confusion. "Why, God, why?" A deep sleep enveloped me. For the rest of the night I didn't have to think about the baby sons I never got to hold.

Sunday was agony for me, listening to the cries of the other babies. But again, I didn't cry. I went home the next day, immediately gathered all the baby things, and I threw them to the back of the closet.

I cried, "What did I do, God? Where were You when I needed You?" God seemed like a Stranger to me, a far-away, unloving Stranger. I knew He existed, but I didn't really know Him at all.

For months my resentment and agony mounted. Neither Jim nor I wanted to see or hear any babies. I didn't want to hold somebody else's baby or see a mother holding her own baby.

The next summer we went to visit Jim's parent and decided to look up some old friends from our courtship days. Jack and Laura greeted us from their front lawn swing. As we exchanged greetings, I became aware of a sickening realization. We didn't know they'd had a baby but now I heard his cries from inside the house.

We had just gotten there. We couldn't just leave. It was now or never. I steeled myself as I walked determinedly into the house and followed the baby's cries to his room. Without hesitating, I picked him up and squeezed him to my chest. A few sobs escaped me. The baby was startled into silence. I quieted my sobs, too, and I allowed the healing process to begin.

After that experience I forced myself to be around babies and hold them. It was hard to do. I still hurt. For two years the bitterness and resentment lingered in my heart. But each time I held a baby the resentment toward God and each mother's baby grew less. I still didn't understand why I wasn't allowed to keep my babies, but I began to see God differently. Hope began to surge in my heart. I didn't have to live in resentment.

Even though my questions remained unanswered, I learned little by little that God truly was "my refuge and strength, a very present help in trouble."

Now as I thought about Dean and Shari's loss, I prayed that they would not turn against God as I had. I prayed that they would allow God to ease their hurt and that they would discover for themselves that regardless of circumstances, God's love and compassion truly never end. God *is* a very present help in trouble.

"Please Stand By"

DONNA CLARK GOODRICH

or months after my mother died, I dreaded each new day and I cried at the least little thing. I knew she was in heaven, but I missed her tremendously. This loss, plus the stress of running a tax and secretarial service and my husband's recent heart attack, had taken its toll.

Discouraged, I felt like God was a thousand miles away. Why wasn't He comforting me? Why didn't He strengthen me more to cope with my difficulties?

One day I stood at the sink doing dishes, trying to pray. Finally I almost shouted, "God, are You there? Can You hear me at all?"

At that very moment from the TV in the living room I heard these words: "The audio portion of our program has been temporarily disrupted. Please stand by!"

What perfect timing! What encouragement! I kept the faith and soon the depression lifted.

Meadowlark Morning

KRISTI G. DUBAY

he air was crisp and clear that autumn morning. I sat on the park bench sifting through the horrifying details of the past few days. The sun warmed my bruised body. I longed for it to comfort my battered soul, but there was no warmth to be found.

Two nights before, my teenage daughter had run away from home. I found out where she was and went to bring her back. As I drove through the night, anger burned inside me as I thought of her rebellious and disrespectful attitude that had controlled our lives for months. I was the parent; she was the child. She would do what I said.

I reached the house where she was staying. Shaking with anger and fear I approached the door. She wouldn't come out so I went in. I was consumed with a fierceness that surprised me. I grabbed her by her long ponytail and dragged her, kicking and screaming, out of the house. Her shrieking obscenities only strengthened my resolve to control her, by force if necessary. I hit her. Then I hit her again. I managed to get her into the van, holding her hair in a death grip—she was not going to get away again. I drove home with her grabbing the steering wheel, punching at my body, trying desperately to get away. Somehow we arrived home, both of us completely out of control. I called our family therapist for advice. She told me I needed to call Child Protective Services to report the incident.

The reality of what happened began to set in. I could not believe I had hit the daughter I loved so much. I was ashamed of my anger. Then I grew alarmed at the prospect of the authorities becoming involved.

The remainder of the night was agony. Wave after wave of guilt and shame flooded over me as I replayed each sickening moment of the night. I couldn't stop my thoughts. *How could I, a Christian mother, have done such a thing? Will my daughter run away again? Will the authorities take my children away? I can't pray, I'm not worthy for God to listen or respond. What I've done is unforgivable.* But my family was in crisis and we needed God to intervene. Was He there?

The soothing melody of a meadowlark perched in the tree above my head called me back to reality. Soon another joined him. Another came and yet another, until the whole tree was filled with a heavenly chorus of birds singing, it seemed, just for me. I knew God was saying, "I'm here to restore your heart and comfort your soul." I sat resting in His love, listening to His precious gift for I don't know how long. As quickly as the meadowlarks came they disappeared.

Then I knew that I could face whatever was to come. The Lover of my Soul was in me. He would walk with me through the consequences of my actions.

I returned home to wait for the caseworker from Child Protective Services. When she arrived I was surprised to see a lovely young woman with a sweet smile. She introduced herself and I invited her in. Entering, she carefully surveyed our home, looking for signs of neglect and abuse. I saw her eyes come to rest on a charcoal drawing of Jesus. Her face lit up and she said, "May I ask you a personal question?" I thought this was strange since she was there to dig into my personal life, but I answered yes, realizing I had nothing to hide.

"Are you a believer?" she asked. I replied that I was and she reached out, gave me a big hug, and said, "You're going to be just fine."

We spent the next hour discussing all that had happened and how our family could approach this "opportunity for growth." She asked the legal questions her job required. Then she began to ask the spiritual questions. "Are you going to church?" "Are you reading your Bible?" "Are you spending time with the Lord?" I realized the answer was no. At that moment I knew I needed to get right with God.

Her job done, the caseworker wrote "No Further Action" on the form, prayed for our family, then left our home. I was in awe. My Heavenly Father had sent a sister, an angel to minister to me and bring me back to Him.

Though more difficult times were ahead of us I had been given a hope that could never be taken away. I had witnessed the Lord's hand at work in my life, not because I was righteous or deserving, but because He loves me. He restored me when I sought His face and repented with all my heart. Psalm 31:7-8 says, "I will be glad and rejoice in your love, for you saw my affliction and knew the anguish of my soul. You have not handed me over to the enemy but have set my feet in a spacious place."

At the moment of my deepest anguish, God sent me a mead-owlark morning.

"What's Wrong, Mommy?"

DAWNETTE KENYON

t had been a long ten months. My husband, Steve, had lost his job because of a "management consolidation." One day I was laboring over our budget to see how to make our ends somehow be on the same page, let alone meet in the middle. With all hope lost, I dropped my head in my hands, and out of pure despair, I began to weep. My tears smeared the ink of the demands of my creditors that beckoned to be paid. It resembled our life. *Everything is distorted and so far out of reach, how will we ever clear it up?*

"What's wrong, Mommy?" my three-year-old son, Brian, asked. His big blue eyes were wide with wonder and concern.

"Oh, Honey," I responded, trying to swallow back the tears, "Mommy is just a little sad right now. I'll be fine."

"Do you want me to pray for you? I'll tell Jesus all about it!" His tiny hand rested on mine. His dimpled fingers and tiny digits held so much more faith in them than mine ever could.

"Sure, Honey. That would be nice. Tell Jesus all about it."

With that, Brian flew to the couch, buried his head in the pillow, and began speaking to Jesus in a language I'm not sure I've ever heard before. There was anguish and genuine tears, petitions and mournful groans. The only thing I could make sense of was, "Jesus! Mommy! Sad! Please, Jesus! Please!" It lasted only about two minutes and then he sat up, wiping away his tears. He gathered himself together, mustered up every ounce of courage his 35-inch, 30-pound body could, marched over to me and said, "There, Mommy. I prayed for you and Jesus will take care of you!" He kissed my tear-stained face and danced away to play without a care in the world.

As I write this, we still haven't found steady employment, but I have something even more precious than any job could provide: a three-year-old who taught his Mommy what it really means to have faith.

Rebound Blessing

FLORENCE FERRIER

 sense of desolation had settled heavily on me about three weeks after my husband Darwin's funeral. I sat alone, opening and reading the day's mail. Sympathy cards were still coming, including one from a city where we'd lived years before, although I didn't recognize the address.

After I'd read the name and the written-in message, I closed my eyes and let the tears splash, remembering our encounters a few years earlier.

When we revisited a city where Darwin had worked a few decades before, some of his former co-workers were still on the job. Leon was the first to greet us. Soon he was telling us about his wife's long battle against cancer, which had ended with her death a few months earlier.

When Darwin was drawn away to greet someone I didn't know, Leon told me how supportive and helpful his extended family had been throughout that difficult time. "But now my friends and even my family members are telling me, 'Get past it . . . get on with your life!' But I *can't* shut off how I feel . . ."

I'd rarely heard a man speak so openly about the journey of grieving. How could I respond to such naked pain revealed by someone I didn't know well? Then these words came to me, "You needn't listen to anyone telling you how long to grieve. There's no formula for how long it takes any one person to heal. But later, when you do find yourself ready to start letting go of it, remember there's *nothing* wrong with that."

Leon blinked a few times as if that were a whole new concept—and thanked me for hearing him out. The next time we traveled through that town, Darwin was talking with someone else when Leon came in. This time Leon greeted me with a genuine hug instead of the usual handshake! Without preamble he said, "You know, I never forgot what you said last time we talked. You can't imagine how that helped me."

234

While I was groping to recall what I could've said, Leon reminded me and then eagerly shared his news. "I'm engaged to Sandi. She's worked here for years. Please come and meet her."

Several Kleenex later, I went back to the note in Leon's sympathy card. He had written: "I know these are difficult times for you. Please use some of the good counsel you gave me a few years ago, which was by far the most meaningful that I received from anyone."

During those intense but brief encounters with Leon years before, what I said had been heartfelt, if not especially memorable. Yet somehow it had come full circle to provide an abundant blessing for me during my own life-changing crisis.

Spiritual Things Are
Spiritually Discerned

VENUS E. BARDANOUVE

y open heart surgery was followed by severe complications and I lay in a coma. For several days there was much medical activity in my room—many doctors, nurses, and others caring for me—but I was unaware of it.

What I do remember in detail was every spiritual experience! The night before the surgery, I was told I would be unable to speak for a few hours after the operation because of a respirator that would be in place. I said to my family members, "I'll feel silly just looking at you. I would appreciate it if some of you would read to me from the Bible during those few minutes you are allowed to come into intensive care."

Visitors were allowed into the room for only five minutes of each hour and only one person at a time. I recall my granddaughter Brigitte coming into the room and saying, "Grandma, I'm going to read Psalm 103 to you out of your Bible." She then prayed for me.

Next, her mother came into the room and said, "Mother, I'm not very good at this, but I want to pray for you." She cried herself through a prayer for my recovery and read Psalm 23 to me. The next hour it was my younger daughter who came in to pray for me and read Psalm 91. I remember all of those visits.

Then after a few more days, my minister son stood by my bed and said, "Mother, I'm going to pray for your healing and I want you to join me." He prayed, and within a few hours I improved and was out of danger. I asked him later if I "joined him"?

He said, "Well, you looked at me."

As I later looked back on my intensive care experience, I understood what I Corinthians 2:14 means when it speaks of spiritual things as "spiritually discerned." I realized that my body was almost dead—but my spirit was alive and well. My spirit had no interest whatsoever in all the voices and activity that surrounded me for those tense days, but responded when there was something of spiritual significance.

Now, when I see a developmentally disabled person or someone in a coma in a hospital, I remember what the Lord taught me about the ability of the human spirit to respond when the body cannot. And I thank God that we are never beyond His abundant love and comfort!

The Important Signpost

JEANNE ZORNES

 he drone of the jet engines clouded my thoughts as I looked out the window at the blanket of cottonballs obscuring the land below. *How appropriate*, I thought, *for my life at this moment. Within days I'll make the biggest decision of my life and God's will is hidden. Should I stay in a job where I'm in a rut but have a dependable salary? Or should I give it all up to raise support for the unknown challenges of missionary life?*

People like me prefer well-marked maps for every turn in life's road. But this next intersection of my life had no reliable signposts. I was proceeding on God's trail markers: the leaning of my heart, the confirmation of Christian friends, and pretty-sure acceptance by the mission. Still the reluctant candidate, I'd spent my Christmas bonus to fly to the mission's U.S. headquarters and check *them* out.

Everything seemed in place, except for my reluctance to jump into change. As a single person, I valued roots and reliability. Why should I quit the known for the unknown? Then, as quietly as clouds swim through the sky, it came to me: "I will instruct you and teach you the way you should go. I will counsel you with my eye upon you" (Psalm 32:8 RSV).

God's eye upon me! The verse I'd read so often in Psalms suddenly gripped me. Maybe I saw little through the airplane window, but God was seeing a lot more. His loving eye was looking from the throne room of heaven, watching that airplane carrying me home. His eye would instruct me through the abundant changes I'd need to make for transitioning to missionary life. What I couldn't see, He could.

Finally I had what I needed for my decision: an affirming word from Scripture. In the following months as I raised support, quit my job, and finally moved to start a short-term mission stint, I often returned to that spiritual signpost from Psalm 34. I didn't need to know everything about what was ahead. God did. And that was enough.

Thanksgiving

It feels so good to be grateful. We can see the benefits of being thankful but sometimes it seems just too hard. Making the choice to be grateful will bring abundant joy into our lives and then we'll be motivated to give thanks—even when we don't feel like it.

All this is for your benefit, so that the grace that is reaching more and more people may cause thanksgiving to overflow to the glory of God.

2 Corinthians 4:15 (NIV)

The Glue of Gratitude

VICKEY BANKS

t had been the hardest year of my life. Grief had been my constant companion. My husband and I had watched two family members die from cancer. Now we were standing in a stark hospital room, listening to the last labored breaths of yet a third one, our dear precious Grandmother.

Up until that time, the phrase "a broken heart" had been just that—a phrase. But now, it was so much more than mere words. It was my reality. I felt the jagged edges of my own heart's pieces as they painfully poked each other. I had never in my life felt such consuming sadness.

I looked into the weary faces of my other family members in that golden-hewed hospital room and saw the weight of emotions pulling on them as well. I saw overwhelming sorrow, helplessness, and confusion over why Grandmother had to linger. *Will this never end?* I wondered. *And, why is my pain so deep?*

Grandmother Banks wasn't my real grandmother, after all. That privilege belonged to my husband. I was not bound to her by blood or childhood memories. However, from the time I married her grandson, she treated me as if I had always been hers. Looking at her frail frame on that cold, hard hospital bed, I was overcome with gratitude for the incredible privilege of having known and been loved by her. Thinking of all the things she had taught me, precious memories flooded my already emotionally overloaded heart. I then did something for which I would always be grateful. I picked up my journal, sat down, and began to put some of those memories on paper.

I wrote words she often said: "You don't say," "Good grief," and "Sure enough." I smiled when I thought of playing in her cherished china cabinet and her pride when she told its stories. She lovingly held her grandmother's faded plate and said, "Someday I want you to take care of it for me." I wrote of us sitting side by side in her big red Cadillac eating hamburgers at the local drive-in and of the day she patiently taught me to make a buttonhole while she actually did all the work!

My pen picked up pace. I couldn't help but giggle about the time everyone thought she was snoring as the Thanksgiving prayer was said—when it was really the sound of the coffeepot! In my mind's eye I once again saw her face light up when she listened to how far I had stretched the Christmas money she always gave us "kids." My mouth watered when I remembered the taste of her chicken and dumplings. And then, I wrote about the greatest thing she ever taught me—how to die with dignity.

I wrote of her uncomplaining spirit and total acceptance of her fate. I remembered the day she told me what it felt like to lie in bed with cancer, and when she admonished me, "If your body grants you any time, it is your responsibility to really live life." I wrote it all down—the memories and the words. And, when I did, something dawned on me. I realized the privilege of loving her was well worth the pain of losing her.

Yes, my heart still hurt, but abundant gratitude for the time we did share became the glue that began to put the broken pieces of my heart back together again.

Hands of Prayer

LES & LESLIE PARROTT

 lbrecht Dürer wanted to paint ever since he was a child. When he was old enough, he left home to study the great art and artists of the world. Along the way, Albrecht became friends with a fellow student who shared his passion for art. As starving artists, the two beginners found it difficult to make a living and study art at the same time. That was when Albrecht's friend offered a tremendous sacrifice—he would work while Albrecht studied. The idea was that once Albrecht's paintings began to sell, his friend would then have his chance.

At first, Albrecht resisted his friend's offer, but after much persuasion he agreed. Albrecht worked faithfully as an artist while his friend toiled long hours to make a living.

The day came when Albrecht sold a woodcarving and his friend went back to his first love. As he began to paint once again, he made a dreadful discovery: the hard work he had done to make a living had stiffened and twisted his fingers. He could no longer paint with skill.

Albrecht was filled with deep sorrow when he learned what had happened to his friend. One day as he was returning home unexpectedly, he heard the voice of his friend praying quietly for him, with his gnarled, toilworn hands folded before him.

It was that image that inspired Albrecht to paint something that has since become world famous. "I can never give back to my friend the artistic skill he sacrificed for me," said Albrecht, "but I can show him how much I appreciate what he did for me by painting his hands, folded in prayer."

Albrecht Dürer's inspired painting is recognized today by millions around the world who are blessed by the image of the classic clasped hands. And friends who know the story behind the painting are doubly blessed by the message.

Finding the Creative
in the Mundane

 once had a job typing mailing labels eight hours a day for a publisher in New York. It had to be one of the most boring jobs on the planet. All day long I sat there typing names and addresses in a room without windows. I realized that if I was going to survive the tedium I had to somehow make the job fun for myself, so I invented a new game every day as I typed. How many labels a minute? How many names starting with M? How many French names? Italian names? Jewish names? How many from Michigan, Minnesota, and so on? I became a rather fast typist through the experience.

Attitudes count more than we think. *Your attitude creates artfulness.* And artfulness expresses more of yourself than you think. The soul feeds on life's experiences and digests them, creating character. Don't rob yourself. Nourish yourself with creative and emotionally satisfying experiences. Even in mundane tasks, release your creative nature to make the difference between boredom and a genuine experience of discovery.

A Greater Law than Murphy's

KIMN SWENSON GOLLNICK

e didn't set out to prove Murphy's Law when we started remodeling our kitchen, but anything that could go wrong *did* go wrong. We discovered water damage under the old cabinets and had to install new subflooring. The countertop wasn't ready when promised. The appliance store called to reschedule delivery of our new oven, requiring us to reschedule the gas company's installation of the now-delayed gas stove. And worst of all, our remodeling contractor asked to be released from his contract—just before Thanksgiving.

There were so many problems plaguing our project I began to wonder if we should expect an invasion of locusts or hordes of frogs. My husband and I decided we'd rather escape our gutted kitchen to share the holiday dinner at my mother's house, or my sister's house, or my brother's house—anywhere but at *our* house. However, it got around that Thanksgiving dinner was still planned at our place because everyone wanted to see our "new" kitchen—finished or not.

Smiling through gritted teeth, I agreed to host it. Nothing like a little extra pressure while adjusting to life with sawdust! On the other hand, I felt a strange desire to share my misery with my extended family.

I ticked off the days, nervously watching The Big One approaching—and still no oven. All my dinner plans hinged on the successful arrival of that oven. In the meantime, we got inventive. We learned how to install kitchen cabinets. Plywood served as a temporary countertop, a nearby bathroom provided running water, and we used paper plates in the absence of a dishwasher. I confessed to my husband that I was getting quite fond of throwing our plates and utensils away.

When our gas stove finally arrived, I started breathing again. Right on schedule and without a hitch, the gas company's technician came out and installed it. It seemed as if we'd finally turned a corner, leaving Murphy's Law and trouble behind. I could almost smell the turkey juices simmering as I slipped into the half-finished room to admire my new appliance.

White enamel gleamed at me, but something wasn't right. My gaze fell on the electronic display and the glass window in the oven door—features I'd wanted but couldn't afford. My mind reeled. It was the wrong model!

What happened? Did the delivery guys pull the wrong box out of their truck? Was my clearance-model oven sitting in someone else's garage while they made frantic phone calls demanding to know what happened?

"I don't need another problem!" I cried. I hit the countertop in angry frustration. All the little problems over the past several weeks overwhelmed me. I broke into tears.

"Lord, you know how much trouble we've already had with this kitchen! In fact, I deserve a little bonus right now. The store probably doesn't even know where the mix-up happened, so they can't trace it to us."

I hardened my heart even as a quiet voice countered my arguments: "But what if they do?"

"It's their problem, Lord. Let them figure it out."

"Is that treating others how you want to be treated?"

"But it's not my fault this happened!"

"How will you explain this when your family comes for Thanksgiving dinner? Will this glorify Me?"

Ouch. That last one hurt.

For a moment I considered whether I could keep it all a secret. I shook my head. I've never been comfortable with hiding things.

I looked with longing at the beautiful oven and let my fingertips lightly touch the display panel. I tried to imagine using it, but recoiled with a pang of guilt. It could never be mine—not without reminding me of my dishonesty every time I used it, day after day, year after year. This oven was beautiful, but it wasn't really mine. I didn't pay for it. Someone else did.

Sighing, I knew this "deep-down-you-know-what's-the-right-thing-to-do" feeling. I didn't like it, but I forced myself to reach for the phone. I dialed the number to the appliance store warehouse. Silently, and with dull resignation, I told God, "This is for You, Lord." Then, and only then, did peace envelope my heart.

When I explained the mix-up on the phone, the employee checked her records. She replied, "No, we delivered the correct one."

I carefully repeated the model number.

"Mrs. Gollnick," she said, "that number is indeed the model you ordered, but it was out of stock on your delivery day. Instead of rescheduling again, we delivered the next model up—at no extra charge. That's our standard policy."

My mouth dropped open.

"Are you sure?" I finally stammered. "Really?"

She assured me it was true. Repeatedly.

I had to make one last call. The salesman in the appliance department confirmed the store's delivery policy. I asked for the price on the upgraded model. It was $200 more than the one we'd ordered.

Chills chased up my spine as I realized a great and awful truth. If I hadn't called the warehouse, I'd have never known about the generous gift God had for me and my family. He knew all along the oven was mine; He'd intended it for me. But I didn't know that. All He wanted was for me to tell the truth—which in essence meant to release what I wanted.

That Thanksgiving while I prepared our holiday dinner, I quietly thanked God for giving me and my family this unexpected and rare gift of abundance. Then I thanked Him for reminding me of a law greater than Murphy's—His loving sovereignty.

Rich Beyond Compare

DENISE A. DEWALD

One day while I was sitting
Feeling sorry for myself,
I started listing my laments
Took my pen down from the shelf . . .

"My stringy hair so needs a perm
My clothes are old and worn;
No money to go shopping with
I'm lonely, bored, forlorn . . .

No close friends to visit with
To share some times of fun;
My days are filled with dull routine
From dawn to setting sun."

But Jesus pricked my heart with shame
And made me think again—
He gave me something new to write,
And words flowed from my pen . . .

"The cancer patient has no hair
And would gladly welcome yours;
Your clothes would warm the homeless one
Whose rags are thin and torn . . .

The money you'd go shopping with
The truly poor could use—
Would you share your wealth, my child . . .
Or spend it as you choose?

The daily chores I've given you
Are blessings sweet and rare;
The paralyzed would love your work
. . . And count each day as fair.

There are lonely People everywhere
Waiting for a friend—
They, too, are bored and need some fun . . .
They're just around the bend."

And now I see things differently—
I'm rich beyond compare!
I've got to run—there's someone near . . .
Who needs to know I care.

Striped Paint
And Other Impossibilities

FREDERICK O. OLSEN

lthough I have never completed a degree, I have attended several universities and trade schools but only long enough to discover what I needed. My natural mechanical ability allows me to make any device I see. I can visualize how wheels, levers, and other mechanical components will affect each other. This talent has served me well in my technician's job at 3M Company.

Engineers there had been struggling to eliminate heat-load failures of Sola-blokâ, a louvered plastic film designed for heat and light control in window glass.

I thought that a louvered plastic sheet or film could eliminate this heat load failure. I surmised that it could possibly be created by fusing a clear plastic layer alternately with an opaque layer into a large log-like chunk with the layers perpendicular to the axis of the piece. If I then cut a thin film from this log the same way the forest industries make plywood, I could end up with a louvered film which would allow me to control light direction like a miniature venetian blind. In theory the idea worked well but when I heated the layered plastic log to forming temperatures, the plastic just flowed around the cutting blade and no film resulted.

One night I prayed, "God, give me the best answer for a technique that will work." His idea came to me: if the plastic log were left at room temperature, the plastic would remain extremely tough. Then the thin surface layer of the billet—heated with an intense energy source—would be pushed off over the knife edge and be much smoother than a film made by extrusion.

3M Company had previously developed a copy machine based on heat-sensitive media. In the spare parts warehouse I found some of the old prototypes of the copy machines along with several pallets of spare heaters for those obsolete models. Enlisting the help of a creative machinist from our experimental shop, we fashioned a cylindrical heat lamp with a very short focal length parabolic reflector which focused all of the lamp's energy on the surface of the plastic log.

Most of the degreed engineers who had been working on the problem thought we were crazy and would not succeed. They had participated in the first failed attempts and could see no way that a mere technician could come up with the key for success. But I had a Divine Consultant and decided by faith to invite the "brass" to the first trial of our new manufacturing process. All my engineer friends thought I had just signed my walking papers. But I knew what my God could do.

All the doubting engineers, my boss, his superior, and the vice president arrived. I switched on the lights and threw the automatic feed on the skiving lathe into gear. From the top of the blade flowed a thin sheet of plastic film with stripes running the length of the material. This first successful attempt resulted in a wide variety of products derived from this new louvered film. They resulted from God-given ideas beyond my education or skills. I am thankful.

Unexpected Blessings

F. ARLINE ZIMMERMAN

breathed a sigh of relief as I settled into my easy chair to read the morning paper on that first day of vacation. It was the summer of 1967, and I was down in Philadelphia after resigning my position as assistant professor of nursing at Goshen (Ind.) College where I had taught public health nursing for a year. My specialty was pediatric nursing, and I had accepted an offer to teach in my area of specialization at Eastern Mennonite College. I anticipated a summer of leisure in my home in Philadelphia, Pennsylvania, before reporting for my new assignment in Harrisonburg, Virginia.

A mild pain pierced my right index finger as I bent it to unfold the newspaper. My arthritis, which annoyed me periodically, had been diagnosed as rheumatoid by a specific test. I was aware that the possibility of a cure was not expected. The physician predicted progressive crippling and suggested that I pursue a doctorate so I could teach nursing, which could be done from a wheelchair. At the present stage, there were periods of relief from pain and swelling of joints, and periods of restricted activity when normal movement made my wrists, fingers, and ankles quite painful. The stabbing pain in my finger that morning reminded me of my predicament.

As I opened the paper, I saw a blaring full-page advertisement of a white sale at Wanamakers Store. I needed sheets and could think of no reason but laziness to ignore the opportunity to economize. I drove toward downtown Philadelphia but felt uneasy. Thinking it was laziness, I chided myself and drove a few more blocks. But I just couldn't shake my uneasy feeling and returned home.

"This is silly," I rebuked myself. "You need sheets, go get them." I again left but experiencing the same uncomfortable feeling compelled me to return home.

As I approached the door, I heard the phone ringing and hurried to answer it. "This is Dr. Hingson and I am calling to invite you to join a group of volunteers for mass immunization programs in Costa Rica. Will you consider it?"

"Yes," I eagerly replied. "I have vacation time coming and I can serve for at least six weeks."

"Great!" he replied. "I have been trying to contact you for the past half hour and this was going to be the last time I called."

I had met Dr. Hingson, founder of Brothers Brother Foundation, in Korea, where he tested his immunization guns in a massive program to protect against measles. After we concluded our conversation, I thought of the unrelenting uneasiness which compelled me to return home. I was relieved to realize that the Lord was the source of it.

Months later in Costa Rica, the leader of my team dispensed preventive medication for malaria. I explained I didn't need any as I had a supply with me left over from my previous trip to India.

Shortly before the end of the program, I developed a fever and mild respiratory difficulty. Months later I learned that I had malaria. I endured the usual episodes of high fever, teeth-chattering chills, and profuse sweating—the classic symptoms of malaria. A blood test showed blood cell destruction. A definite diagnosis of malaria was made after consultation with a physician who had served in the tropics.

As the months passed, I waited for my usual arthritic activity to begin and was grateful for the extended period of pain-free joints. Another winter came and went. I began to suspect that something unusual had occurred. Months turned into years and the arthritis did not return.

Years later in Philadelphia I discussed the situation with co-workers, one a physician from the Communicable Disease Center on assignment in Philadelphia. He informed me that malaria was considered a possible cure for arthritis but that research was limited and not approved. The cure could be more life threatening than the arthritis.

Each rainy day or during a snowstorm, I flex my pain-free fingers and thank God for deliverance from rheumatoid arthritis. I'm eternally grateful for the prompting of the Holy Spirit which caused me to return to my home to get the call for service in Costa Rica, as well as for the outdated pills for malaria I had on hand. It's a good thing I didn't check the expiration date on the bottle. As a nurse, I was ashamed of my negligent nursing practice but perhaps my mistake was also the abundant will of God for my deliverance from rheumatoid arthritis.

I eventually got my doctorate but not my wheelchair.

A Depression with a Blessing

RUTH GIAGNOCAVO

he years from 1929 to 1939 are known in our country as the Great Depression, or by some as "the lost years." Unlike most brides of her acquaintance in those years, my mother began her married life in an apartment in a small town instead of a farmhouse. My father had steady work as a truck driver for a local quarry company. My mother was happy in their cozy place which had all the modern conveniences.

In less than two years after their marriage, my grandmother needed a farmer for one of her farms. My mother and father were her logical choice but my mother was dismayed! She didn't want to leave her modern conveniences for a big, rambling farmhouse with no electricity and no running water. Nevertheless, they moved to the farm.

My parents bought the necessary livestock and equipment in the spring of 1929, and by the Fall after the stock market crash, their assets were worth a great deal less than when they had begun the year.

Seven years passed and the family grew to nine young children. Two sets of twins made the group seem even larger. My mother often said, "As long as I have butter, eggs, and cream, I can always cook." And she did.

However, there was always the reminder of those bleak and harsh years. Tramps—homeless men who came by our farm— asked for a place to sleep and a hot meal. We even had our "own" regular tramp, named Shorty, who made the trip through our area every spring and fall. Sometimes one of the tramps would offer to do a chore such as painting or chopping wood in return for a homemade meal and a bed in the haymow.

Occasionally, a car would stop and the "town" people would tell my parents how fortunate we were. It was true! We weren't poor—we just didn't have any money. The cows gave milk, the chickens surrendered eggs, and there was always the abundant garden in the summer. Regardless of whether there was an abundance or a lack, we always paused for grace before meals.

My mother often told us, "At the time, I didn't welcome moving from the bright, comfortable apartment with all the conveniences to the old farmhouse. But now I see how God provided for all of us during those darkest of times. The move to the farm with room to grow food *and* children turned out to be the greatest blessing of all."

Celebration

$\mathcal{F}$rom the beginning of God's interaction with man, He encourages His people to enjoy times of celebration. He knows how much we need such stress-relievers and wants us to rejoice in His abundant love and provision for us.

So all the people went to Gilgal and confirmed Saul as king in the presence of the LORD. There they sacrificed fellowship offerings before the LORD, and Saul and all the Israelites held a great celebration.

1 Sam 11:15 (NIV)

The Lord's Supply of Himself

RUSSELL J. COX

t was a tough time. We knew accepting the pastorate of a relatively new church comprised of people from several different backgrounds would be an opportunity—even a challenge. However, we did not expect to receive promised salary checks intermittently. The present intermission had lasted for six weeks.

Without employment, reserves, or support from the outside, our grocery supply ran out with no means of replenishing it. The five mouths of our family were not eating as regularly as usual, and none of us felt called to a forty-day fast!

At the time and ever since, we are not certain what or how much we ate. We do know that without food in the pantry or refrigerator, we lived without hunger and without loss of vigor or joy. There were occasions when we sat at the table with only a bowl of rice for which to thank the Lord. Although there was "not enough" for all of us, we rose from the meal with our hunger satisfied. At other times, there wasn't even rice!

After what we assuredly believed to be a miracle of living *on* faith, "by faith" a lady from the congregation contacted us in the seventh week.

"We buy whole sides of beef to stock our deep freezer, but none of our family likes prime rib. Do you folks eat prime rib?"

What do you say to a question like that? "No. But only because we do not have any." Or, "Oh, yes; it's part of our regular diet." Or, "We would sure like to try." Or, "Hallelujah!"

How do you react? With an assumed attitude that is calm, cool, and collected? Or with a shout?

I am not certain what we said or how we said it. I do know there was unbridled gratitude to our Lord and to our friend for her sensitivity.

Because we did not have sufficient gas in the car to pick it up, we were thankful for her delivery of the meat the next day. Along with the meat, she placed a box of fresh vegetables on the table, saying, "My two sons sent these from their gardens. I hope you can use them."

My wife was already planning the feast with which to surprise our three daughters when they returned from school. But the Lord wasn't through! He knew the meal needed more. Our friend opened her purse and pulled out two checks.

"My sons have made some money by working part time and by selling some produce, and they are learning how to give to God as good stewards. They felt the Lord wanted you to have this money."

When the Lord sets the table, He sets it with grace, abundance, and class. Grateful and excited, we received His bounty. It would sustain our physical life for a while. Whether He gives prime rib or not is not the issue He addressed for us. Instead He revealed, "There are times you'll live 'on' faith and discover that I alone am enough—even abundant."

God's Gift

BARBARA J. ANSON

ittle did I know when I recorded, then promptly forgot, a simple prayer, how abundantly God would answer five months later. It all began while I was recovering from a broken ankle one rainy day near the end of winter.

In a wistful state of mind, I wrote in my prayer journal, "Wouldn't it be fun to have a three-day vacation with Orris? Lord, I'm dreaming of a 'real' vacation, not our typical visit with relatives. It would be so nice to spend a few days alone, just the two of us."

My mind wandered back to our mountain honeymoon and how much fun we had that week in July a few years earlier. Lazy days of sailing and sightseeing had often ended with evening barbecues under the stars. If only we could escape again for a few days to a peaceful place.

Orris had recently changed from contract to employee status with his company but didn't have any vacation time coming. After being on crutches, then in a walking cast, I longed to be out of the house and in new surroundings. But my wistful desire seemed too far out of reach to even mention to Orris. Yet, I knew God would understand the longing of my heart.

Time passed, and in June, Orris traveled to England on business. How I longed to go with him. A week in England would have been a wonderful vacation, but God was preparing an even better plan. I had forgotten my simple vacation prayer, but God hadn't.

One day Orris called from England. He explained, "Honey, I'm going to be returning to England in July and you can probably go with me. This next trip will be longer—maybe two weeks. That will give us a free weekend to explore on our own." I couldn't believe my ears! What a delightful prospect!

By the time Orris came home, the projected two weeks in July had become a month. We would be staying in a picturesque historic town where I could spend the work week going on long walks in the peaceful countryside and delving into the origins of my family name in the local library.

Our month in England turned out to be a precious gift from the hand of God, a present that kept unfolding day after day with perfect weather, lunches beside a meandering river, afternoons in a quaint 17th-century hotel courtyard surrounded by an abundance of beautiful flowers, and dinner at sidewalk cafes. Weekends were vacation times together as we explored the Isle of Wight, London, Windsor, Oxford, Stratford-on-Avon, and even a little village that bears my family name, Barrington. History came alive as we visited castles, palaces, cathedrals, and churches. God even blessed me with new friends when I joined in a mid-week Bible study at a local church.

Looking back, I am awed by how abundantly God answered a simple prayer, going far beyond anything I could have asked for or even dared to imagine. By the way, did I mention that our only expenses that July were a few souvenirs and photographs?

First Things First

KATHY PEEL

en years ago I had a radical, life-altering experience. When our boys were aged eleven, seven, and
six months, my life was chaotic. It's not that it had
been smooth sailing up to that point. It's just that
the older boys were all of a sudden in the sign-up-for-every-sport-
and-activity-offered years, and we were getting used to having a
baby around again. I was so busy, running from meetings, to appointments, to ball games, to events, to luncheons, and nursing
the baby in between, that I was starting to forget important things-
like depositing paychecks in the bank. Like making sure we had
milk for breakfast. Like picking up the carpool after school. I was
overwhelmed, exhausted, and ultimately I landed in the hospital.

After undergoing numerous medical tests, I was diagnosed with
chronic mononucleosis syndrome. (Today this is called chronic
fatigue syndrome.) I was completely drained of energy and unable to think clearly or function without pain. During the six
hours a day I managed to hold my eyes open, I did a lot of thinking.

I thought about how I got myself into this miserable state. Was
it because my calendar was booked to eternity? Was it because I
had said "yes" to everyone who asked me to do anything? All of
the above were true. Maybe my doing so much wasn't the cause
of my illness, but I got sicker because I ignored the warning signs
and didn't take care of myself.

I closed my eyes and relived the day prior to my crash. In addition to the responsibilities of running my own home, I had attended two community-service meetings, cooked and delivered
dinner to two new mothers, helped a friend frost her hair so she
could save fifty dollars, and met another friend at a store to help
her pick out clothes for a trip—all with my six-month-old in tow.
I suppose everyone has a day like that every once in a while, but
for me, that was typical.

As I lay in bed, I also thought about how I would spend the hours of the day if the gift of time were given back to me. I decided I would not merely spend time doing this or that, I would use time for things I felt were important. Thankfully, my health and my time eventually were restored. Since then, I've never been the same. I see each day as a gift, undeservedly given to me to use as best I know how, and I've learned to manage my time pretty well.

Passport to Hospitality

MARILYN RYAN

*A*ll I want to do is feed the needy!" I stated, frustrated. "It's Easter, have a heart."

But the park department official was adamant. "Sorry, Ma'am, but we don't permit functions of that type in the park. Now, if you want to have a family gathering, that's one thing. But huge crowds? Sorry, against the regulations."

I hung up the phone, fuming. We weren't going to charge a fee or solicit anything. We just wanted a friendly celebration with games, good conversation, and lots of food. I took my frustration and anger to the one place I was sure of finding comfort—God.

"Dear God," I prayed, "I've always wanted to serve a good meal to the needy in the park, but the park board says no! What should I do to change the park official's mind?" No answer came! I was perplexed. I tried in vain to reason with God, even to strike a bargain, but to my disappointment, no answer popped into my mind.

I sighed. *I guess I'll just keep on cooking food, anyway. Is that the answer?* I didn't know for sure.

With that thought in mind, I started a marathon of baking, planning, and cooking. My guest list wasn't large—my daughter and Mike, Mike's brother and his family, Mike's Dad and family, and another close friend, Bill, who was fighting his last bout with cancer. Still I found myself cooking as if for a multitude. How were we going to eat all this food—especially since my daughter and the other families all planned on bringing additional dishes of their own?

Easter Sunday dawned slightly cloudy, windy, and cool. My husband, John, left for the park early, to reserve a spot. He was to set the tables with paper plates, silverware, and napkins.

I loaded the van, making numerous trips back and forth. I loaded a huge stuffed turkey, a large ham, sweet potatoes, cranberry sauce, homemade rolls, and pies! Lots of pies! At the last minute Cindy tapped my shoulder.

"Umm, Mom, I hope you don't mind, but we invited some people from our church to come and eat with us. They had no place to go."

"When will they get there?" I asked, mentally reviewing the amount of food we had. Would it be enough? I decided we had plenty to feed a few extra.

"Actually, they'll be coming with the pastor."

"You invited the Pastor too? Well, okay. We have lots of food."

"Just one more thing . . . I think he invited some people, too."

I wondered how many *some* people would be, but didn't really worry. There was a lot of food in that van!

We arrived at the park and began to unload the food. People trickled in, some toting more food, others simply bringing their appetites. The kids started a ball game while adults rearranged the picnic tables. My mind was in a whirl, trying to keep the names and faces straight as I was introduced to each new couple. Cindy's pastor arrived, lugging folding chairs and more hungry people.

We gathered around the table, praised God for the food we were about to eat, and were just dipping in, when I noticed a family of three walking nearby. They looked wistfully in our direction. Impulsively I called out to them, "Come join us!" They grabbed some paper plates and piled them high.

Not long after, another poor-looking family appeared out of nowhere and asked if they could join us, too. After I said "of course!" they disappeared, and returned minutes later, scrubbed up and ready to eat.

As we enjoyed the bounty, I talked with the two families who had joined us. Tales of unemployment, hunger, and despair poured out. I packed a hefty bag of leftovers for the two families, and thrust a few dollars in their hands. Tears trickled down my cheeks as they left.

Suddenly, as I looked over the crowd who had assembled that chilly Easter afternoon, I realized I had gotten exactly what I had asked God for: I had fed the needy, we'd all had pleasant conversation and played a few games. *Best of all*, I thought, *I kept to the park official's regulation. After all, aren't we one big family in God? He directed my mind and actions all the way.*

Exhausted, I retreated home after loading the van and mentally thanking God for His abundant hospitality.

Point of Light,
Or Do Cats Ponder Stars?

HOWARD THOMPSON

own through the centuries, man has been very curious. He has wondered about the heavens, the earth, the sea, and countless other unfathomable mysteries. Of course, over those many years of exploring and learning, mankind has managed to answer at least some of the riddles and questions of life. However, I don't believe my questions have been answered yet.

It was about eleven o'clock in the evening when I drove into my wooded front yard. The headlights picked out shrubs, trees, and the tall, dark, lamppost I had forgotten to turn on, four hours earlier.

As I came around this certain shrub, the headlights connected with the glowing eyes of my two best buddies. Smokey, a black cocker spaniel, was bounding off the porch, and on his heels, maneuvering for position, came PeeWee, a yellow fluff-ball of an orphaned cat, given to me by a friend.

There was a sliver of a moon providing some light but when I stepped out of the car, I reached down, picked up the cat so I wouldn't step on him, and started walking toward the front door. He always liked being carried like a newborn baby and tonight was no different.

Hopeful no one would hear me, I asked him as I often did, "Well, how's PeeWee tonight? Have you been having fun with Uncle Smokey?"

As I stopped for a moment to scratch the cat's ears and to let my eyes adjust to the semi-light, I looked up at the twinkling sky. Looking back at me were Orion, the Big Dipper, Jupiter, and countless other points of light.

Continuing my journey to the front door—and as silly as it must sound for a grown man—I asked the cat if he was ready for bed. He made his customary sound. Sort of a grunt/purr. I looked at him and saw his two big eyes staring upward over my shoulder. I followed his line of sight but could see nothing but millions of stars.

I stopped walking once more, and asked, laughing at myself, "Do you like the stars, too, PeeWee? Do you ponder them?" He made that sound again: grunt/purr.

I looked back to the sky then at the cat. He was still staring up with an expression of silent wisdom . . . a million stars reflected in his eyes.

So there I was. A dog at my feet, quietly waiting for whatever was going on to end, and a cat in my arms who was checking out the heavens. At that moment, I wondered, a little sheepishly, if any of the millions of pet owners in the world had ever shared star watching with their pets.

At the front porch, I put PeeWee down, unlocked the door, and entered the house. As I sat down, preparing to watch what was left of the news, I kept thinking about the response from PeeWee. In that brief moment outside, was I not the one pondering and my cat the Sage? In those few minutes, he and I were joined at a point of light that shone elsewhere in other skies.

I turned off the TV and went to bed. I lay there for awhile, sleepily thinking about my pets, and the role they play in my life. Their antics make me laugh, their attention lowers my blood pressure, and their quiet companionship is a gift to my soul. Although I had no answers to my questions, I was consoled by the revelation that PeeWee and I together are indeed part of the whole.

As my eyes began to close, I was humbled greatly by God's awesome plan. I whispered, "Thank you."

I also thanked PeeWee, who was by now, far out of range of my voice . . . chasing a mouse or cricket, or doing other cat things in the starlit night. I thanked him for the brief moment when man and creature shared some sort of understanding in the design.

If I am allowed more of these times, I pray I will recognize them in their rare—but abundant—occurrence.

A Long Winter

EDNA MAST

ne morning as I went to work at the elementary school where I was an instructional aide, I found everyone in shock. A fire had leveled a mobile home the night before, leaving the family homeless; several of the children attended our school. Our staff made immediate emergency plans to receive money, food, clothing, or whatever the family could use.

I wanted to help, but what could I do? I couldn't take time to drive home to put together a box of food or dig out some bedding. And after school I needed to drive to Lancaster General Hospital where my husband Alvin was a patient following a near-fatal farm accident. He now needed skin grafting from his knee to his ankle.

I checked my wallet, thankful that my next paycheck was due in a few days. I found a five-dollar bill among a few ones. I quickly tossed it into the basket and went about my work.

The day dragged its feet. As I left the building that afternoon, a sharp autumn wind brought a chill. I hurried to my car and shivered, thinking that it would be a long winter, not only for my family but also for the family without their home. As I drove the twenty-five miles to Lancaster, my spirit plummeted into worry about the future's uncertainties. But once I'd "hit bottom," I realized I could only look *up*.

I did that, stopping at a restaurant for a bowl of soup and a hot drink because I only had a few dollars left. As I entered the dining room, I noticed friends of ours, a pastor couple, trying to get my attention. As I approached their table he said, "Join us. We've just ordered. Order what you want; it's on us."

She added, "Ever since we heard of Alvin's accident, we wanted to do something for you. Here's our chance."

I thanked them, sat down, and enjoyed an hour of uplifting fellowship and a warm meal.

All at once, I chuckled as I told them of my experience that morning. "God is returning my small gift with 'interest.' He does that, but not usually this soon!"

My friends were blessed in giving and I received a double blessing that day. Now I could go to the hospital and encourage Alvin as I shared my day with him.

He was hospitalized for two months and disabled for six months. I took an extended leave of absence when he returned home. Not being a nurse, I learned how to care for his injuries. During that time I learned many faith-building lessons.

The church where we served gave us their annual Christmas offering; their gift paid our overdue tax bill. Our fire company brought us a Christmas turkey for our family dinner. Two groups came Christmas Eve and caroled, one leaving a fruit basket. After our family members left on Christmas Day, Alvin took his first few steps, unaided. Goodbye walker, crutches, and wheelchair!

A young couple, friends of one of our sons, came and stayed for a few days, bringing us January cheer. When the fuel oil truck made a delivery, he grabbed the bill and paid it. On one of the coldest days in February, a schoolteacher friend volunteered to chauffeur us for an appointment with our orthopedic surgeon.

I remember one day placing my flat wallet on the table and saying, "God, you know." Money came with cards, from visitors, local organizations and church groups.

We welcomed spring with thankful hearts. Months earlier I had feared the future. Now, I looked back and thanked God for the abundance of that long winter. What I didn't want to face had become unforgettable blessings to be celebrated.

Grace On Ice

KAREN O'CONNOR

'll never forget my tenth birthday. My father came home early from work and picked me up from school, his new black leather ice skates slung over his broad shoulders and my new white ones in his hand. "We're going down to the pond to skate," he said, "just the two of us. It's my birthday present to you."

The mere thought of having my father all to myself brought tears to my eyes. He worked long hours in those days and it was rare that he took time off for leisure.

I waved good-bye to my friends and piled into our old tan car. Off we went to the nearby pond, now frozen hard after a week of sub-freezing temperatures. I wrapped a wool scarf around my neck, pulled my stocking cap over my long brown hair and donned my mittens. Then hand-in-hand, Dad and I skated over and around the pond all afternoon. Whenever I hit a bump or felt scared, he was there, stretching out his hand to hold me up and to guide me through the maze of skaters whizzing by.

As the sun began to set, we piled into the car and drove home, our noses red and our cheeks cold. But our hearts were bursting with warmth—for one another, for the fun we had, for the celebration of my tenth birthday.

I skated many times after that but none meant as much to me as that special day with Dad alone. Then unexpectedly a few weeks ago one of my granddaughters invited me to her tenth birthday party. The afternoon would include lunch at a favorite restaurant and indoor ice skating at a local rink.

I said, "yes," to lunch, but "no" to skating! "I haven't skated in forty-five years," I told Sarah. "I'd be scared to go out on the ice after such a long time. But I'll have fun watching you and your friends from the bench."

For the rest of the week, however, I wrestled with my decision. "You're not a sit-on-the-sidelines kind of grandma!" I told myself. "You're a tree-climbing, peak-bagging, color tag-playing grandmother."

I wanted to skate. But I was afraid. Back and forth I went. Yes, one day. No, the next. The Saturday morning of the party I made up my mind! I would get out on the ice and see what happened.

When it was time to skate, I gulped hard, held onto the guard rail the first time around, then took a deep breath and stepped out into the whirl of skaters whizzing past me. "If only Dad could be with me," I whispered. I swiped at the tears that trickled down my cheeks. My father is 92 now and in a wheelchair.

"Oh Lord," I prayed, "help me do this. For some reason I really want this victory." Before I uttered the last word I realized I was skating—really skating. The more confident I felt, the faster I went, round and around, excited by this new-found freedom.

There was my heavenly father upholding me, as my earthly father had done so many years before. Fear vanished as the truth of God's promise in Isaiah swept across my mind and encouraged my heart. "For I am the Lord, your God, who takes hold of your right hand and says to you, Do not fear; I will help you." (Is. 41:13 NIV)

I was new in that moment of God's love and provision. If he would uphold me in a simple thing like ice skating, surely he would be there for all the big challenges in my life. From that point on, I promised the Lord and myself that I would step out— at home, at work, in my community—without hesitation, for I know without a doubt that my heavenly father is holding my right hand. How abundant are the blessings of our gracious Lord.

My Sweet Gum Miracle

D.J. NOTE

 struggled to dig two holes in the black soil on either side of our barnyard gate. Several salty beads of perspiration trickled down the side of my face. For months my husband neglected to plant my sweet gum trees as he had promised. One tree still appeared healthy, but the second had succumbed to the confines of its tiny bucket. As I lifted the lifeless little trunk from the container, the last tentacles of root tore away. "If only he had kept his promise," I thought, shoving the dehydrated stump into the hole. I pushed the dirt up around the tree covering its base with the suffocating sticky soil. Secretly, I hoped guilt would overcome my husband when he saw the dead tree—now planted. A reminder of his unkept promise.

For nearly a month, I watered and pampered the remaining tree, completely ignoring the dried torso sticking out of the ground on the opposite end of the gate. Then one day I noticed tiny, bright-green foliage clinging to the base of the dead tree's trunk. My mind struggled to believe what my eyes couldn't deny. Without fanfare, God had resurrected the lifeless tree. And without water! I threw my arms into the air in grateful worship, but just as suddenly I felt utterly humbled.

Until now, the bitterness I felt toward my husband for his unkept promise had consumed me. I felt small and ashamed, like Adam and Eve must have felt in the garden when they tried to run and hide. In spite of my anger, God was demonstrating his love for me. It was the first time I realized that God truly cares about even the small, insignificant things in my life. And He's bigger than all my frustrations and fear.

"Oh, Father, forgive me," I whispered. "I've been so angry."

Over the next few months, I cared for both trees. But as the tiny resurrected tree flourished, despite all my efforts, the other healthy tree slowly withered and died. Then one day in the quiet of my mind I recognized His voice. "Man's labors will vanish, but that which I bring forth is sustained."

I didn't replant another tree in place of the one that died. Not as a memorial to my husband's broken promise, but this time as a reminder to me of my own lack of forgiveness. And our 20-foot sweet gum tree thrives today, a testimony to us both of God's unfailing mercy and love.

Contributors

Nora Lacie Abell, a writer, lives on the Colville Confederated Tribes Reservation. Her experiences as a wife, health care professional, mother, and tree farmer give her a unique perspective on rural America. Contact: Long Rifle Ranch, Inchelium, WA 99138.

Charlotte Adelsperger, speaker and author of two books, is thankful for husband Bob and grown children, John Adelsperger and Karen Hayse, who is also a writer. Charlotte's articles and poetry have appeared in 70 publications. Contact: 11629 Riley, Overland Park, KS 66210, (913) 345-1678.

Debbie Allen is a freelance writer/editor whose work has appeared in many books, magazines, and newspapers. A new mom, she is now working on children's books. Contact: 44 Catskill Avenue, Rensselaer, NY 12144, (518) 434-5829. E-mail: alleneditor@att.net

Barbara J. Anson is a wife, mother, grandmother, and former dental hygienist. A speaker and writer, she has a heart for encouraging Christian women in the practical application of Biblical truths. Contact: 1415 Tom Fowler Dr., Tracy, CA 95376. E-mail: oanson@pacbell.net

Marie Asner is a poet, writer, and entertainment reviewer in the Kansas City area. She won the Grand Prize in writing from the 1998 Kansas City Christian Writers Conference. E-mail: HALMAR9999@aol.com

Marlene Bagnull is a wife, mother of three adult children, and author of six books. She directs the Greater Philadelphia and Colorado Christian Writers Conferences, teaches writing seminars, and ministers to caregivers of aging parents. Web site: http://nancepub.com/cwf/

Vickey Banks is a wife, mother, and inspirational speaker with CLASServices, Inc. She is also a freelance writer and the author of the upcoming book, *Love Letters to My Baby*. Contact: 6400 Sudbury Drive, Oklahoma City, OK 73162, (405) 728-2305. E-mail: Vbinokc@aol.com

Venus E. Bardanouve, a retired speech pathologist, has published in many Christian periodicals and books. She also authored *Monologues for Ministry* and two Bible study guides, *All the Angels in the Bible* and *When the Almond Tree Blossoms*.

Martine G. Bates is a freelance writer specializing in educational, Christian, and travel writing. She has a wealth of experiences to draw from, having been a school principal, mayor of a small town, and mother of two sons.

Margarita Garza de Beck is a freelance writer who also pastors "Cristo la Roca," an Hispanic outreach of the church where she and her husband are members. Contact: 58 Denwood Dr., Jackson, TN 38305. E-mail: margaritabeck@msn.com

Ellen Bergh speaks from her platform of pain that God turned to gain. Her marriage moved from gall to glory. She and CB own Mastermedia Publishing and oversaw the High Desert Christian Writers Guild's first book in '98. E-mail: mastermedia@hughes.net

Pam Bianco is a wife, mother, aspiring speaker, and writer for numerous Christian magazines, including *Virtue, Woman's Touch, Just Between Us* and many web publications. Contact: 11549 Pepper Way, Reno, NV 89506, (775) 677-0904. E-mail: TapestryWM@aol.com

Joan Rawlins Biggar lived in Alaska for 17 years. She is a former teacher and author of two book series for young people, *Adventure Quest* and *Megan Parnell Mysteries* (Concordia Publishing House). Contact: 4425 Meridian Avenue N. #3, Marysville, WA 98271.

Christy Brewster lives on the beautiful Oregon coast with her husband and two children. She writes for ministry and family publications. E-mail: christyb@popmail.com

Jan Brunette has been a minister's wife for 17 years, mother of 4, the stepmother of 7 and the grandmother of 20. Her articles appeared in *The Lutheran Witness, Resource, Baptist Leader,* and many other publications. She has taught in Christian schools for 13 years and is active in her Sunday School program and women's organization.

Barbara Bryden lives in the Pacific Northwest with her husband, Ken, and eccentric cat, Bozo. She works as a freelance writer and spends a great deal of time with her grandchildren, gardening, and reading. E-mail: dvff75b@prodigy.com

Charlotte H. Burkholder is a freelance writer, married, mother of four, grandmother of six. She is a graduate of the Christian Writer's Guild and has had a number of articles published. Contact: 2128 Eversole Road, Harrisonburg, VA 22802, (540) 434-2907. E-mail: mrb@cfw.com

Sue Cameron enjoys writing, worship dance, drama, and serving at Christian writers conferences. She also likes her husband, Craig, who is an orthopedic oncologist, their four children, and new daughter-in-law. Contact: 13200 Ashvale Drive Fairfax, VA 22033. E-mail: smcameron@juno.com

Sandra Palmer Carr is a wife, mother and grandmother, and a member of the Christian Writer's Fellowship of Orange County. She gives hope in Jesus through poetry, stories, drama, and devotionals. Contact: 9421 Hyannis Port Drive, Huntington Beach, CA 92646-3515, (714) 962-0906.

Arlene Centerwall lives in beautiful B.C. Canada and has had several true short stories and poems published in books and magazines. She spends time writing and is involved with Asiaalive, which takes the gospel to Asia. E-mail: ARLENE CENTERWALL@ bc.sympatico.ca

Laraine E. Centineo is a wife, mother and grandmother, who enjoys writing, painting, reading and walks along the ocean. Her husband recently retired. They thank God for spending more time together. Contact: 2417 Riverside Terrace, Manasquan, NJ 08736, (732) 223-2858. E-mail: WriterL@aol.com

Joan Clayton and husband, Emmitt, are retired educators. Her passion is writing. Emmitt's is ranching. Joan is working on her sixth book. She is also the Religion Columnist for her local newspaper. Joan and Emmitt reside in Portales, New Mexico.

Valerie L. Baker Clayton is in full-time ministry with Youth With A Misson. She has served in Ukraine, Hawaii, and Virginia. The mother of seven, she is a speaker and has just published her first book, *Answering My Heart's Cry.*

Mary L. Cotton, a retired English teacher, likes to read, write, swim, bicycle, and sing. She and husband Seth spend summers in Michigan and winters in Florida. They enjoy short mission trips abroad. Contact: 1060 Meadowbrook, White Cloud, WI 49349.

Russell J. Cox writes for periodicals and presents weekend seminars on Christian character and early morning prayer. He lives with his wife, Dolores. Contact: 1238 West Myrna Lane, Tempe, AZ 85284-2833, (602) 592-9241. E-mail: russdeecox@juno.com

Doris C. Crandall, an inspirational writer, lives in Amarillo, TX. Co-founder of the Amarillo Chapter of Inspirational Writers Alive!, a group dedicated to Christian writing, Doris devotes much of her time to helping beginning writers hone their skills.

Anesa C. Cronin, a Christian for 17 years, has a BA in Sociology, two Master degrees in Counseling Psychology and Correctional Counseling, and two Credentials. She has traveled overseas extensively and has been published. Contact: 5824 Thornhill Drive, Riverside, CA 92507, (909) 781-4260.

Pat Curtis, besides writing Christian stories, also writes for children. She and her husband, Max, are now retired and reside with their little Yorkie, Skeeter. Contact: 2517 Ohio Ave. Joplin, MO 64804. E-mail: mcurtis@4state.com

Linda Cutrell is a new writer who is inspired to write on her day set apart with the Lord, where she fasts from the world. She has sold articles to *Decision, Joyful Woman, Celebrating Life, Purpose* and *Expressions.* Contact: 5370 East Forster Ave., Columbus, IN 47201.

Denise A. DeWald aims to encourage the hurting with her writing. She loves her family, camping, and old books. She's published books, anthologies, devotionals, and she's been aired on Family Life Radio. Contact: 1744 Swenson Rd, Au Gres, MI 48703-9412, (517) 876-8718.

Kristi DuBay is a wife and mother of three. She lives in Albuquerque, NM and is active in Women at Calvary ministries. Kristi has learned the value of sharing the stories of her life to encourage others.

Jean Ann Duckworth, M.Div., is an author and speaker. She lives with her husband, Terry, and daughter, Katy. Contact: 520 S. Grand St., Orange, CA 92866, (714) 633-2654. E-mail: Revwriter @aol.com

Karen Dye is a wife and mother who leads women's Bible studies and worship at her local church. Contact: P.O. Box M, Lone Pine, CA 93545, (760) 876-5465.

Irene Faubion has been married to Wayne for 61 years. She has two daughters, four grandchildren, and ten great-grandchildren. After serving 40 years in pastoral work, she now teaches English pronunciation. Contact: 335½ Monterey Rd, So. Pasadena, CA. 91030.

Florence Ferrier lives near Baudette, MN, close to the Canadian border. She is a former social worker, now doing volunteer work in addition to her freelance writing. Her work has appeared in over 45 magazines plus other publications.

Jo Franz is a freelance writer whose stories have been published in a number of books and magazines. She shares God's love, hope, and joy through her speaking and singing for conferences, retreats, churches, schools, women's groups and banquets. E-mail: Jofranz@aol.com

Rudy Galdonik speaks about her experiences of having open-heart surgery at age 25, of buying a near-bankrupt business, and of being wid-

owed at 43. Using humor, she encourages audiences to put perspective on life's struggles. Contact: (401) 885-4209.
E-mail: Rudywg@aol.com

Ruth Giagnocavo and her husband owned a bookstore for over 20 years. She lives in Akron, PA and is the mother of 7 children and grandmother of 12. She has had poetry published in Christian publications. This is her third contribution for Kathy Collard Miller.

Verda Glick praises God for abundantly providing for her family during 33 years of missionary service in El Salvador. Her book, *Deliver the Ransom Alone*, tells of her husband's kidnapping. Part of that story appeared in *Guideposts*. E-mail: glorias@vianet.com.sv

Nancy Godbehere is a wife, mother of three, grandmother of eight and an active member of Christ Lutheran Church in Phoenix, AZ. She is the personal assistant to Naomi Rhode, the professional speaker. Contact: 11645 N. 40th Place, Phoenix, AZ 85028, (602) 953-8234.
E-mail: njgodbeh@smarthealth.com

Kimn Swenson Gollnick started her writing career as a performer, writing comedy routines to share truths from God's word through ventriloquism. Now she's a wife, mother, award-winning writer, and conference speaker. Web site: http://home1.gte.net/gollnick.
E-mail: gollnick@gte.net

Donna Clark Goodrich, of Mesa, AZ, is the author of 17 books and over 700 articles. An instructor at writing seminars, she also types, edits, and proofreads manuscripts. She and her husband, Gary, have three children and two grandchildren. E-mail: Dgood648@aol.com

Glenda Gordon is a social worker who occasionally freelances as a writer and graphic designer. Contact: 3633 North Pole Lane, Riverside, CA 92503, (909) 278-0952.

Teresa Griggs of Sikeston, Missouri, has experienced God's peace and comfort through the loss of her daughter, Mallory. She actively shares God's message of hope as she speaks to women across the country.
E-mail: griggs@bootheel.net

Beverly Hamel went to San Diego, CA, from Kansas City, MO, via the US Navy and stayed after her enlistment was completed. She's been married to her husband, Gary, since 1977. She has taught a mixture of Southeast Asian children for over 10½ years.

Lee Hill-Nelson has been a Texan all her life except for 20 months as a US Navy WAVE, in WWII. She is now a retired church secretary, freelance writer, grandma, Mom, wife, and tutor. She writes personal experiences, travel pieces, and children's stories.

Dawnette Kenyon and her husband, Steve, have been married since May, 1983, and they have three children. A retreat and conference speaker, Dawnette's goal is to edify, equip, and train women to reach their full potential in Christ. E-mail: dawnettekenyon@juno.com

Lettie J. Kirkpatrick is a homemaker, freelance writer, and women's conference leader. She and her husband, Tom, live with their four sons. Contact: 373 Charles Circle, Cleveland, TN 37323, (423) 479-2063.

June Cerza Kolf retired after 12 years of hospice work. The author of five books relating to grief, she writes for inspirational magazines and has over 125 published articles. Currently, when she and her husband are not traveling, they enjoy their four grandchildren.

Jane Koning lives in Southern California with her husband, Fred. They have four grown children and three grandchildren. Writing a weekly letter for five years to her Bible Study Fellowship class in the local women's prison stimulated her interest in writing.

Tina Krause is a wife, mother of two grown sons, and "Nana" to Ian James. She is an award-winning newspaper columnist, speaker, and freelance writer. Since 1990, she has over 650 published columns, editorials, and magazine articles. E-mail: tinak@netnitco.net

Helen Luecke is co-founder and president of Inspirational Writer's Alive! Amarillo Chapter. She has been published in numerous Christian magazines and devotional books. She lives in Amarillo, Texas, with her husband, Richard.

Edna Mast is a retired teacher and former editor who began writing while serving on the staff of her high school paper. Married for 62 years, she and her husband Alvin have five children plus grandchildren and great-grandchildren. Contact: 250 West Colebrook St., Manheim, PA 17545.

Mayo Mathers is a columnist for *Virtue Magazine*, contributing editor for *Today's Christian Woman*, and a contributing author to eight books. She is also the co-author of *Like a Pebble Tossed–The Legacy of a Prayer* (ACW Press). She has published many articles. Contact: 20129 Mathers Road, Bend, OR 97701. E-mail: mathers@bendnet.com

Ruth E. McDaniel is a freelance writer, novelist, poet, caregiver to her husband since 1991, frequent writing instructor, mother, and grandmother. She seeks to spread God's love to a hurting world. Contact: 15233 Country Ridge Dr., Chesterfield, MO 63017.

Kathy Collard Miller is wife, mom, speaker and best-selling author of 35 books including *God's Vitamin "C" for the Spirit* and *God's Abundance for Women*. She speaks 40 to 50 times a year nationally and internationally. E-mail: Kathyspeak@aol.com

Lynn D. Morrissey, author of *Seasons of a Woman's Heart*, is in *Why Fret That God Stuff?* and *Teens Can Bounce Back*. She is a CLASSpeaker on prayer-journaling and women's topics. Contact: 155 Linden Ave., St. Louis, MO 63105, (314) 727-8137. E-mail: lynnswords@primary.net

A. Jeanne Mott, a former flight attendant, teaches ESL to K-12 foreign students. Writing has been her passion since early childhood, and she is published in many Christian periodicals and books. Contact: P.O. Box 550183, Gastonia, NC 28055. E-mail: ajwrite@ibm.net

Deena L. Murray, a public speaker and women's ministry director, lives in Corona, CA with her husband and foster children. She is editor of *Sharing Hope & Joy* published by Caring Hearts Ministry, (909) 279-9224. E-mail: murray@pe.net

Deborah Sillas Nell lives with her husband, Craig, and daughter, Sophia. She is a freelance writer, artist, and counselor. Contact: 735 McAllister St., Hanover, PA 17731, (717) 637-4065.

Janie Ness, wife to fireman Doug and homemaker to three teenagers, finds great pleasure in writing. She has been published in *God's Vitamin "C" for the Hurting Spirit* and *Why Fret That God Stuff?* Contact: 11118 N.E. 124th Ave., Vancouver, WA 98682.

Doris Hays Northstrom, four years after a divorce, married a classmate she met at her 45th high school reunion picnic. She enjoys teaching creative writing, juggling the joys of two families, playing tennis, biking, and gardening with her new husband, Ron.

D. J. Note, a member of Oregon Christian Writers and Mom's In Touch International, contributes regularly to *Cascade Horseman* magazine as well as national publications. Her love of God, family, and country life inspire her writing. E-mail: djnote@juno.com

Karen O'Connor is a popular speaker at retreats and conferences and an award-winning author of 37 books including *Basket of Blessings: 31 Days to a More Grateful Heart*. Contact: 2050 Pacific Beach Drive, #205, San Diego, CA 92109, (619) 483-3184. E-mail: wordykaren@aol.com

Frederick Olsen, a recent graduate of the Institute of Children's Literature, has been a researcher for 3M for 33 years. He is a math tutor, a longtime storyteller, a husband, father, and grandfather. He has four children and seven grandchildren. Contact: 1127 Gresham Ave. N., Oakdale, MN 55128-5811, (651) 739-8966.

Golden Keyes Parsons is a speaker, writer and musician who enjoys speaking at women's events. Her husband, Blaine, joins her to lead marriage conferences as well. Contact: P.O. Box 764, Red River, NM, 87558. E-mail: bgpar@taosnet.com

Nancy E. Peterson has also been published in *God's Abundance—365 Days to a Simpler Life*, two of the *God's Vitamin "C"* books, and *Why Fret That God Stuff?* Contact: 28626 Tulita, Menifee, CA 92584, (909) 679-5137.

Jennifer Botkin Phillips, "social commentator" and radio talk show host, has appeared on MSNBC, ABC-TV, WCBS Radio and others. She is president of JBP Media Relations, a consultant, and a motivational speaker. Contact: P.O. Box 123, Montvale, NJ 07645.
E-mail: Jenleetalk@aol.com

Lois Erisey Poole, a freelance writer and author of *Ring Around the Moon*, is published in numerous senior papers including *Oblates, Senior Expressions, Senior Voice,* and *Elder Update*—published by the state of Florida. Contact: 2607 W. M-8, Palmdale, CA 93551-0402.

Laura Sabin Riley is a wife, mother, passionate speaker, and author of *All Mothers Are Working Mothers* (Horizon Books), a devotional book for stay-at-home moms, and numerous short stories. Contact: P.O. Box 1150, Yuma, AZ 85366. E-mail: RileysRanch@juno.com

Carol Russell, a Sunday school teacher for 41 years, speaks to women in classes and fellowship meetings. She is a member of the Pittsburg Christian Writers Fellowship in Pittsburg, KS and the KCCN in Olathe, KS.

Marilyn Ryan and her husband reside in Phoenix, AZ, where she enjoys music, reading, writing and volunteer work. A nostalgic Christian writer, her work has appeared in *Good Old Days, Mature Living, The End,* and *Cheerful Times.*

Terry Fitzgerald Sieck is a professional public speaker and author. She and her husband, Larry, live in San Diego. Contact: (619) 549-1074.
E-mail: LSieck@Pacbell.net.

Debra West Smith, a wife and mother of two teenagers, enjoys travel, history, and teaching Sunday School. Debra's published works include the Hattie Marshall series and numerous magazine articles. Contact: 9158 Arnold Rd.,Denham Springs, LA 70726.
E-mail: dlwsmith@juno.com

Ronica Stromberg has worked as a newspaper reporter, a marketing assistant, and most recently, an editor for an educational corporation. She now works at home, caring for her sons, and writing freelance pieces.

Patty Stump, a vivacious speaker who communicates Biblical truths with humor, insight, and practical application, is a popular retreat and Bible study leader. She has also contributed to several books and is a Christian counselor. Contact: PO Box 5003, Glendale, AZ 85312, (602) 979-3544.

Alena Stutsman, a graduate of St. Paul Bible Institute (Crown College) and Wisconsin State College (University) in River Falls, is a former elementary school teacher and a writer of poetry, devotionals, and stories. Her work has appeared in various publications. E-mail: sastutsman@integrityol.com

Howard Thompson, a native of Buffalo, NY, moved to Florida in 1946 and now resides in Apopka, FL with his wife Sandra and three cats. Retired from the construction industry, he pursues short-story writing as a part-time vocation.

Marcia Van't Land is the author of *Living Well With Chronic Illness* and is available for speaking engagements, including women's retreats. Contact: 12648 Ramona, Chino, CA 91710, (909) 627-2024.

June L. Varnum writes articles, devotions, and a little poetry. She enjoys amateur photography, walking, and reading. June has also taught Sunday School and led Bible studies, prayer groups, and retreat workshops. Contact: P.O. Box 236, Loyalton, CA 96118, (530) 993-0236. E-mail: jvarnum@psln.com

Joel R. Waldron Sr. is a graduate of Bristol University at Kingsport, Tennessee. A full-time evangelist, Joel has been in the ministry for 40 years and has written articles for newspapers and magazines.

Lori Wall, a single parent with three children, is a published playwright/writer and in-house playwright for Exodus Theatre Troupe. She is self-publishing a poetry book to minister to AIDS victims. Contact: PO Box 41-701, Los Angeles, CA 90041, (626) 585-1305.

Phyllis Wallace is a wife, mother, family counselor, author, educator and the host of Lutheran Hour Ministries' popular radio program, "Woman to Woman." Contact: 2185 Hampton Ave. St. Louis, MO, 63139. E-mail: W2w@lhm.org

Martha B. Yoder, who was forced from nursing by post-polio problems, writes articles for Christian Light Publications. She has done nine Children's Story Tapes for Gospel Sunrise Ministry. Contact: 1501 VA Ave. Apt.159, Harrisonburg, VA 22802, (540) 564-6560.

F. Arline Zimmerman taught pediatric nursing, served in Korea and India for five years, and worked for 20 years in school health administration. She continues her service to others through the Rambo Committee-Sight for Curable Blind-India. Contact: 108 Hill Road, New Holland, PA 17557.

Jeanne Zornes' ministry outreach, "Apple of His Eye," emphasizes spiritual encouragement and growth. A humorous, Biblically-focused speaker, she's written five books, including *When I Felt Like Ragweed, God Saw A Rose* (Shaw). Contact: 1025 Meeks, Wenatchee, WA 99801, (509) 663-1953.

Note: To the best of our knowledge, all of the above information is accurate. In some cases, we were unable to obtain biographical information.

—The Starburst Editors

Credits

Some stories in *Stories of God's Abundance* come from other books, which are credited below in order of their appearance in this book. You will find these stories in this book on the page numbers noted at the end of each entry.

Abundant Love In A Little House from *It's About Home*, Patsy Clairmont, Servant Publications, MI, 1998. Used by permission.

Theology Of Basketball adapted from *If I'm Not Tarzan, And My Wife Isn't Jane, Then What Are We Doing In The Jungle?*, Steve Farrar, Multnomah Press, OR, 1991. Used by permission.

Building Anticipation from *Let Her Know You Love Her*, Bill Farrel, Harvest House, OR, 1998. Used by permission.

Unconditional Love from *Romancing the Home*, Ed Young, Broadman & Holman, TN, 1994. Used by permission.

Positive Stress from *On Becoming a Real Man*, Edwin Louis Cole, Thomas Nelson, TN, 1992. Used by permission.

Going Beyond Acceptance from *The Gift of Family*, Naomi Rhode, Thomas Nelson, TN, 1991. Used by permission.

Toss It Into The Lake from *Tough Times Never Last, but Tough People Do!*, Robert H. Schuller, Crystal Cathedral Ministries, 1983. Used by permission.

Abundant Peace from *Lord, I Want to Know You*, Kay Arthur, Multnomah Books, OR, 1992. Used by permission.

The Sonar Fish Finder, The Day My Plate Was Broken from *On the Anvil*, Max Lucado, Tyndale, IL, 1985. Used by permission.

Dirty Windows from *Eternity*, Joseph M. Stowell, Moody, IL, 1995. Used by permission.

Here Comes the Groom from *Only Angels Can Wing It*, Liz Curtis Higgs, Thomas Nelson, TN, 1995. Used by permission.

Door-to-Door Service from *Mirror, Mirror on the Wall, Have I Got News for You*, Liz Curtis Higgs, Thomas Nelson, TN, 1997. Used by permission.

Making People Feel Special from *How to Make People Really Feel Loved*, Charlie W. Shedd, Servant, MI, 1996. Used by permission.

Two War-Time Miracles from *Miracles Happen When You Pray*, Quin Sherrer, Zondervan, MI, 1997. Used by permission.

A Surprise Ending from *Detours, Tow Trucks, and Angels in Disguise*, Carol Kent, NavPress, CO, 1996. Used by permission.

A Treasured Legacy from *Laugh Again*, Charles Swindoll, Word, TN, 1991. Used by permission.

Run After Him from *A Graceful Waiting*, Jan Frank, Servant, MI, 1996. Used by permission.

Hungry for God from *Breaking Through*, Wellington Boone, Broadman & Holman, TN, no copyright given. Used by permission.

Stick It Out Till June from *You Don't Have to Quit*, Anne & Ray Ortlund, Thomas Nelson, TN, 1986,1988, revised 1994. Used by permission.

Letting Go To Be Free adapted from *A View from the Porch Swing*, Becky Freeman, Broadman & Holman, TN, 1998. Used by permission.

Other Good Choices from *Empowered by Choice*, Kendra Smiley, Servant, MI, 1998. Used by permission.

Risky Grace from *The Grace Awakening*, Charles R. Swindoll, Word, TN, 1990. Used by permission.

Going Home from *Because of Love*, William & Patricia Coleman, Servant, MI, 1998. Used by permission.

Flickers of Hope from *Mama, Get the Hammer!*, Barbara Johnson, Word, TN, 1994. Used by permission of author.

"Adios, Ross" from *Half Time*, Bob Buford, Harper Collins/Zondervan, MI, 1994. Used by permission.

Hands of Prayer from *A Good Friend*, Les & Leslie Parrott, Servant, 1998. Used by permission.

Finding the Creative in the Mundane from *A Confident, Dynamic You*, Marie Chapian, Servant MI, 1997.

First Things First adapted from *The Family Manager*, Kathy Peel, Word, TN, 1996. Used by permission.

Other Books by Starburst Publishers
(Partial Listing - Full List available upon request)

Stories of God's Abundance—for a More Joyful Life
Compiled by Kathy Collard Miller

Find joy, inspiration and insight, turn to these beautiful, real-life stories written by people who share their stories of how God has changed their lives. Renew your faith in life's small miracles and challenge yourself to allow God to lead the way as you find the source of abundant living for all your relationships.
(trade paper) ISBN 892016060 **$12.95**

God's Abundance
Edited by Kathy Collard Miller

This day-by-day inspirational is a collection of thoughts by leading Christian writers such as Patsy Clairmont, Jill Briscoe, Liz Curtis Higgs, and Naomi Rhode. *God's Abundance* is based on God's Word for a simpler, yet more abundant life. Learn to make all aspects of your life—personal, business, financial, relationships, even housework a "spiritual abundance of simplicity."
(cloth) ISBN 0914984977 **$19.95**

Promises of God's Abundance
Edited by Kathy Collard Miller

Subtitled: *For a More Meaningful Life*. The Bible is filled with God's promises for an abundant life. *Promises of God's Abundance* is written in the same way as the best-selling *God's Abundance*. It will help you discover these promises and show you how simple obedience is the key to an abundant life. Scripture, questions for growth, and a simple thought for the day will guide you to a more meaningful life.
(trade paper) ISBN 0914984-098 **$9.95**

God's Unexpected Blessings
Edited by Kathy Collard Miller

Learn to see the unexpected blessings in life. These individual essays describe experiences that seem negative on the surface but are something God has used for good in our lives or to benefit others. Witness God at work in our lives. Learn to trust God in action. Realize that we always have a choice to learn and benefit from these experiences by letting God prove His promise of turning all things for our good.
(cloth) ISBN 0914984071 **$18.95**

Why Fret That God Stuff?
Edited by Kathy Collard Miller

Subtitled: *Stories of Encouragement to Help You Let Go and Let God Take Control of All Things in Your Life*. Occasionally, we all become overwhelmed by the everyday challenges of our lives: hectic schedules, our loved ones' needs, unexpected expenses, a sagging devotional life. *Why Fret That God Stuff* is the perfect beginning to finding joy and peace for the real world!
(trade paper) ISBN 0914984-500 **$12.95**

The God's Vitamin "C" for the Spirit™ series has already sold over 250,000 copies! Jam-packed with stories from well-known Christian writers that will enlighten your spirits and enrich your life!

God's Vitamin "C" for the Spirit™
Kathy Collard Miller & D. Larry Miller

Subtitled: *"Tug-at-the-Heart" Stories to Fortify and Enrich Your Life.* Includes inspiring stories and anecdotes that emphasize Christian ideals and values by Barbara Johnson, Billy Graham, Nancy L. Dorner, and many other well-known Christian speakers and writers. Topics include: Love, Family Life, Faith and Trust, Prayer, and God's Guidance.
(trade paper) ISBN 0914984837 **$12.95**

God's Vitamin "C" for the Spirit™ of WOMEN
Kathy Collard Miller

Subtitled: *"Tug-at-the-Heart" stories to Inspire and Delight Your Spirit.* A beautiful treasury of timeless stories, quotes, and poetry designed by and for women. Well-known Christian women like Liz Curtis Higgs, Patsy Clairmont, Naomi Rhode, and Elisabeth Elliott share from their hearts on subjects like Marriage, Motherhood, Christian Living, Faith, and Friendship.
(trade paper) ISBN 0914984934 **$12.95**

God's Chewable Vitamin "C" for the Spirit™ of MOMs
Delightful, insightful, and inspirational quotes combined with Scripture that uplifts and encourages women to succeed at the most important job in life—Motherhood.
(trade paper) ISBN 0914984-942 **$6.95**

God's Vitamin "C" for the Hurting Spirit™
Kathy Collard Miller & D. Larry Miller

The latest in the best-selling *God's Vitamin "C" for the Spirit* series, this collection of real-life stories expresses the breadth and depth of God's love for us in our times of need. Rejuvenating and inspiring thoughts from some of the most-loved Christian writers such as Max Lucado, Cynthia Heald, Charles Swindoll, and Barbara Johnson. Topics include: Death, Divorce/Separation, Financial Loss, and Physical Illness.
(trade paper) ISBN 0914984691 **$12.95**

God's Vitamin "C" for the Spirit™ of MEN
D. Larry Miller

Subtitled: *"Tug-at-the-Heart" Stories to Encourage and Strengthen Your Spirit.* Compiled in the format of best-selling *God's Vitamin "C" for the Spirit,* this book is filled with unique and inspiring stories that men of all ages will immediately relate to. Contributors include: Bill McCartney, Larry Crabb, Tim Kimmel, Billy Graham, Tony Evans, and R. C. Sproul, to name a few.
(trade paper) ISBN 0914984810 **$12.95**

God's Vitamin "C" for the Christmas Spirit™
Kathy Collard Miller & D. Larry Miller

Subtitled: *"Tug-at-the-Heart" Traditions and Inspirations to Warm the Heart.* This keepsake includes a variety of heart-tugging thoughts, stories, poetry, recipes, songs, and crafts.
(cloth) ISBN 0914984853 **$14.95**

God's Chewable Vitamin "C" for the Spirit™

Subtitled: A Dose of God's Wisdom One Bite at a time. A collection of inspirational quotes and Scriptures by many of your favorite Christian speakers and writers. It will motivate your life and inspire your spirit. You will chew on every bite of God's Chewable Vitamin "C" for the Spirit.
(trade paper) ISBN 0914984-845 $6.95

God's Chewable Vitamin "C" for the Spirit™ of DADs

Subtitled: *A Dose of Godly Character, One Bite at a Time.* Scriptures coupled with insightful quotes to inspire men through the changes of life. This little "portable" is the perfect gift for men of all ages and walks of life. It provides the encouragement needed by Dad from time to time.
(trade paper) ISBN 0914984-829 **$6.95**

Seasons of a Woman's Heart—A Daybook of Stories and Inspiration
Compiled by Lynn D. Morrissey

A woman's heart is complex. This daybook of stories, quotes, scriptures, and daily reflections will inspire and refresh. Christian women share their heartfelt thoughts on Seasons of Faith, Growth, Guidance, Nurturing, and Victory. Including Christian women's writers such as Kay Arthur, Emilie Barnes, Luci Swindoll, Jill Briscoe, Florence Littauer, and Gigi Graham Tchividjian.
(cloth) ISBN 1892016036 **$18.95**

More of Him, Less of Me
Jan Christensen

Subtitled: *A Daybook of My Personal Insights, Inspirations & Meditations on the Weigh Down™ Diet.* The insight shared in this year-long daybook of inspiration will encourage you on your weight-loss journey, bring you to a deeper relationship with God, and help you improve any facet of your life. Each page includes an essay, Scripture and a tip-of-the-day that will encourage and uplift you as you trust God to help you achieve your proper weight. Perfect for companion guide for anyone on the Weigh Down™ diet!
(cloth) ISBN 1892016001 $17.95

Beanie Baby® Stories
Susan Titus Osborn and Sandra Jensen

The FIRST and ONLY Beanie Baby® Book that is NOT just a price catalog! Adults and children share their stories and trivia knowledge of those collectable, lovable, squeezable Beanie Babies® with the world. This book includes wonderful, inspiring Beanie Baby® stories from collectors of all ages and quotable quotes as only kids can give them. A book which surely will touch your heart, just as Beanie Babies® have!
(trade paper) ISBN 1892016044 **$10.95**

The Fragile Thread
Aliske Webb

From the author of the critically acclaimed, *Twelve Golden Threads* (over 75,000 sold), comes a novel of one woman's journey through a mid-life transformation as she decides to open a quilt shop in a small town. The novel portrays Aggie, a woman taking risks, facing self-doubts, and reaching out to others. She rediscovers her values, beliefs, and spiritual foundation when a megacorporation threatens to takeover her small town.

(cloth) ISBN 0914984543 **$17.95**

If I Only Knew . . . What Would Jesus Do?
Joan Hake Robie

Subtitled: *Over 100 Ways to "Walk the Walk" and "Talk the Talk"*. In what direction are you walking? Is it in His direction? And how about what you're saying? Would He say it? The phenomenon, *WWJD?* (*What Would Jesus Do?*) is sweeping the country, and this book looks at the fundamental teachings of Jesus and brings them back to life for today's living. The *WWJD?* phenomenon began with a rekindled interest in the 1800's biggest selling book, *In His Steps,* by Charles Sheldon (over 22 million copies). *If I Only Knew . . .* includes timely questions, poignant answers and Scripture.

(trade paper) ISBN 091498439X **$9.95**

If I Only Knew What Jesus Would Do?—For Women
Joan Hake Robie

Finally a *WWJD?* just for women! Today's woman is faced with more life choices and decisions than ever before. The author follows up on her successful book, *If I Only Knew...WWJD?* with a look at the lives of today's women. Get the right perspective—Jesus' perspective—for the day-to-day aspects and challenges of life.

(trade paper) ISBN 1892016087 **$9.95**

A Woman's Guide To Spiritual Power
Nancy L. Dorner

Subtitled: *Through Scriptural Prayer*. Do your prayers seem to go "against a brick wall?" Does God sometimes seem far away or non-existent? If your answer is "Yes," you are not alone. Prayer must be the cornerstone of your relationship to God. "This book is a powerful tool for anyone who is serious about prayer and discipleship."—Florence Littauer

(trade paper) ISBN 0914984470 **$9.95**

Parenting With Respect and Peacefulness
Louise A. Dietzel

Subtitled: *The Most Difficult Job in the World*. Parents who love and respect themselves parent with respect and peacefulness. Yet, parenting with respect is the most difficult job in the world. This book informs parents that respect and peace communicate love, creating an atmosphere for children to maximize their development as they feel loved, valued, and safe. Parents learn authority and control by a common sense approach to day-to-day situations in parenting.

(trade paper) ISBN 0914984667 **$10.95**

The World's Oldest Health Plan
Kathleen O'Bannon Baldinger

Subtitled: *Health, Nutrition and Healing from the Bible*. Offers a complete health plan for body, mind and spirit, just as Jesus did. It includes programs for diet, exercise and mental health. Contains foods and recipes to lower cholesterol and blood pressure, improve the immune system and other bodily functions, reduce stress, reduce or cure constipation, eliminate insomnia, reduce forgetfulness, confusion and anger, increase circulation and thinking ability, eliminate "yeast" problems, improve digestion, and much more.
(trade paper) ISBN 0914984578 **$14.95**

The God's Word for the Biblically-Inept™ series is already a best-seller with over 100,000 books sold! Designed to make reading the Bible easy, educational and fun! This series of verse-by-verse Bible studies, Topical Studies and Overviews mixes scholarly information from experts with helpful icons, illustrations, sidebars and time lines. It's the Bible made easy!

The Bible—God's Word for the Biblically-Inept™
Larry Richards

An excellent book to start leaning the entire Bible. Get the basics or the in-depth information you are seeking with this user-friendly overview. From Creation to Christ to the Millenium, learning the Bible has never been easier.
(trade paper) ISBN 0914984551 **$16.95**

Revelation—God's Word for the Biblically-Inept™
Daymond R. Duck

End-time Bible Prophecy, expert Daymond Duck leads us verse-by-verse through one of the Bible's most confusing books. Follow the experts as they forge their way through the captivating prophecies of Revelation!
(trade paper) ISBN 0914984985 **$16.95**

Daniel—God's Word for the Biblically-Inept™
Daymond R. Duck

Daniel is a book of prophecy and the key to understanding the mysteries of the Tribulation and End-Time events. This verse-by-verse commentary combines humor and scholasticism to get at the essentials of scripture. Perfect for those who want to know the truth about the Antichrist.
(trade paper) ISBN 0914984489 **$16.95**

Health and Nutrition—God's Word for the Biblically-Inept™
Kathleen O'Bannon Baldinger

The Bible is full of God's rules for good health! Kathleen Baldinger reveals scientific evidence that proves the diet and health principles outlined in the Bible are the best for total health. Learn about the Bible Diet, the food pyramid and fruits and vegetable from the Bible! Experts include: Pamela Smith, Julian Whitaker, Kenneth Cooper, and TD Jakes.
(trade paper) ISBN 0914984055 **$16.95**

Men of the Bible—God's Word for the Biblically-Inept™
D. Larry Miller

Benefit from the life experiences of the powerful men of the Bible! Learn how the inspirational struggles of men such as Moses, Daniel, Paul, and David parallel the struggles of today's man. It will inspire and build Christian character for any reader.
(trade paper) ISBN 1892016079 **$16.95**

Women of the Bible—God's Word for the Biblically-Inept™
Kathy Collard Miller

Finally, a Bible perspective just for women! Gain valuable insight from the successes and struggles of such women as Eve, Esther, Mary, Sarah, and Rebekah. Interesting icons like: Get Close to God, Build Your Spirit and Grow your Marriage will make incorporating God's Word into your daily life easy.
(trade paper) ISBN 0914984063 **$16.95**

What's In the Bible for™ Teens?
Mark R. Littleton

From the creators of the *God's Word for the Biblically-Inept*™ series comes a brand new series called *What's In the Bible for…*™. The first release is a book that teens will love! *What's In the Bible for*™ *Teens* contains topical Bible themes that parallel the challenges and pressures of today's adolescents. Learn about Bible Prophecy, God and Relationships and Peer Pressure in a conversational and fun tone. Helpful and eye-catching "WWJD?" icons, illustrations and sidebars included.
(trade paper) ISBN 1-892016-05-2 **$16.95**

On The Brink
Daymond R. Duck

Subtitled: *Easy-to-Understand End-Time Bible Prophecy.* From the author of *Revelation* and *Daniel—God's Word for the Biblically-Inept*™, *On The Brink* is organized in Biblical sequence and written with simplicity so that any reader will easily understand end-time prophecy. Ideal for use as a handy-reference book.
(trade paper) ISBN 0914984586 **$11.95**

Purchasing Information
www.starburstpublishers.com

Books are available from your favorite bookstore, either from current stock or special order. To assist bookstore in locating your selection be sure to give title, author, and ISBN #. If unable to purchase from the bookstore, you may order direct from STARBURST PUBLISHERS. When ordering, enclose full payment plus shipping and handling as follows: Post Office (4th Class)—$3.00 (Up to $20.00), $4.00 ($20.01-$50.00), 8% ($50.01 and Up); UPS—$4.50 (Up to $20.00), $6.00 ($20.01-$50.00), 12% ($50.01 and Up); Canada—$5.00 (Up to $35.00), 15% ($35.01 and Up); Overseas (Surface)—$5.00 (Up to $25.00), 20% ($25.01 and Up). Payment in U.S. Funds only. Please allow two to three weeks minimum (longer overseas) for delivery. Make checks payable to and mail to: STARBURST PUBLISHERS, P.O. Box 4123, LANCASTER, PA 17604. Credit card orders may also be placed by calling 1-800-441-1456 (credit card orders only), Mon-Fri, 8:30 a.m. to 5:30 p.m. Eastern Stan-